DANIEL

UNLOCKED

by

MICHAEL JARVIS

THE COVENANT PUBLISHING CO. LTD.

2014

First Edition 2014

ISBN 978-085205-115-3

Printed by

THE COVENANT PUBLISHING COMPANY LIMITED
121, Low Etherley, Bishop Auckland,
Co. Durham, DL14 0HA
www.covpub.co.uk

Introduction

Daniel was among the captives of Judah that were taken to Babylon. He was among those taken in the first invasion and deportation by Nebuchadnezzar in about 607 BC. The Ten Tribes of the Kingdom of Israel together with many from the Two Tribes of the Kingdom of Judah, had been taken captive by the Assyrians more than a century earlier.

He quickly became a trusted minister under Nebuchadnezzar, and later to Darius and Cyrus, holding office despite political changes and even conquest.

He and his friends had ups and downs because of the jealousy of other officials, but were always vindicated because of absolute faith in God, whom they continued to serve in a pagan land.

His writings fall into two types, his witness to the power and faithfulness of God is in both. First his service to kings, and second, to recording Visions and Prophecies for the then distant future that were 'sealed' or encoded in such a way that they would be only partially understood until these latter days.

The Messages to us that are encoded into his Visions bear a close resemblance to parts of the book of *Revelation*, showing us that the inspiration for it is like Revelation of Divine origin, and the sealed nature of Daniel's Visions are better understood because the Risen Christ broke the seals of the Revelation Scroll.

In this exposition which contains some well understood parts of Daniel's Prophesy, together with personal views as is common in other works, the most important is the reading, direct from the Bible, of those historical records and writings by Inspiration or Command from the Holy Spirit, which accompanies each section without which understanding is not possible.

Michael Jarvis

Cover design using models available on special order.
Details from Covenant Publishing.

Chapter 1

1:1-5.   In the third year of the reign of Jehoiakim king of Judah came Nebuchadnezzar king of Babylon unto Jerusalem, and besieged it.

And the Lord gave Jehoiakim king of Judah into his hand, with part of the vessels of the house of God: which he carried into the land of Shinar to the house of his god; and he brought the vessels into the treasure house of his god.

And the king spake unto Ashpenaz the master of his eunuchs, that he should bring certain of the children of Israel, and of the king's seed, and of the princes;

Children in whom was no blemish, but well favoured, and skilful in all wisdom, and cunning in knowledge, and understanding science, and such as had ability in them to stand in the king's palace, and whom they might teach the learning and the tongue of the Chaldeans.

And the king appointed them a daily provision of the king's meat, and of the wine which he drank: so nourishing them three years, that at the end thereof they might stand before the king.

King James Authorised Version

Daniel was among the first captives from Judah to be taken to Babylon. We shall see that his ministry as a Prophet was a long one, he probably lived to at least ninety. Some suppose he was a prince, but this is uncertain as no lineage is given to connect him with the house of David, even so it will be seen that he was of an aristocratic family, well educated, and an able communicator, which skills would reward him well.

Nebuchadnezzar having captured vessels from the Jerusalem Temple placed them for safe keeping in the secure vaults of his own temple. He chose this course instead of using them in his palace, thus he did not, possibly on the advice of Daniel, deliberately desecrate them, (as did Belshazzar some years later).

Nebuchadnezzar was an astute man and wished to take advantage of the skills and learning of his captives. We may wonder why he should want to do that, many victors would just use them all as slaves. Was it because he hoped to gain from the fabled wisdom that had been the wonder of the world in Solomon's day? Did he think that the best educated and high ranking young men of Judah would still have that secret wisdom? If so, he wanted it, and was prepared to give by his own standards, a good deal to those who would be profitable to him.

1:6-10.   Now among these were of the children of Judah, Daniel, Hananiah, Mishael, and Azariah:

Unto whom the prince of eunuchs gave names: for he gave unto Daniel the name of Belteshazzar; and to Hananaiah, of Shadrach; and to Mishael, of Meshach; and to Azariah, of Abed-nego.

But Daniel purposed in his heart that he would not defile himself with the portion of the king's meat, nor with the wine which he drank: therefore he requested of the prince of the eunuchs that he might not defile himself.

Now God had brought Daniel into favour and tender love with the prince of the eunuchs.

And the prince of the eunuchs said unto Daniel, I fear my lord the king, who hath appointed your meat and your drink: for why should he see your faces worse liking than the children that are of your sort? then shall ye make me endanger my head to the king.

Nebuchadnezzar had given instructions that the captives be screened to select those of high intelligence, knowledge of any science and special skills. These were to be put on a crash course to make them fluent in Chaldee, (Hebrew had already many similarities with Chaldee) and familiar with all things Babylonian. They were then to appear before the king who would interview them and determine their future work. Clearly the king was determined to use the best of Judah to his advantage.

When Daniel and his three friends arrived at the training centre, they were given new names, but Daniel decided that he would not give up his Faith and the Laws of God, this included the food laws, which Jews regard to this day. He therefore regarded Babylonian food as unclean, especially meat, so he requested that he and his friends be given alternative vegetarian foods. This created a rather tricky situation, for the king had already determined the standard of living of his trainees, and stipulated certain foods and wines. Failure on the part of the official to give the proper allowance to his charges, and the king hearing a complaint about it, er - well, the king had no reputation for tolerance or any leniency whatever towards those who disregarded his orders, but Daniel had his way for a successful trial period and they were allowed to continue with their chosen diet. When these four were sent for by the king, he quickly saw that they were superior in wisdom, intelligence and integrity and were destined to hold the highest offices. This will soon be seen to be a wise policy, when the king will show his distrust of his usual wise men.

1:11-16. Then said Daniel to Melzar, whom the prince of the eunuchs had set over Daniel, Hananaiah, Mishael, and Azariah,

Prove thy servants, I beseech thee, ten days; and let them give us pulse to eat, and water to drink.

Then let our countenances be looked upon before thee, and the countenance of the children that eat of the portion of the king's meat: and as thou seest, deal with thy servants.

So he consented to them in this matter, and proved them ten days.

And at the end of ten days their countenances appeared fairer and fatter in flesh than all the children which did eat the portion of the king's meat.

Thus Melzar took away the portion of the meat, and the wine that they should drink; and gave them pulse.

At no time did Daniel interfere with the normal processes of the Babylonian State, by either seeking to impose his own ideas, or offer advice to his monarch to influence him unless asked to do so. A striking contrast to those who thought it clever to use the king's ear to advantage themselves until he found them out, and it was only because of the faithfulness of these four men that the duplicity of others was exposed.

1:17-21. As for these four children, God gave them knowledge and skill in all learning and wisdom: and Daniel had understanding in all visions and dreams.

Now at the end of the days that the king had said he should bring them in, then the prince of the eunuchs brought them in before Nebuchadnezzar.

And the king communed with them; and among them all was found none like Daniel, Hananaiah, Mishael, and Azariah: therefore stood they before the king.

And in all matters of wisdom and understanding, that the king enquired of them, he found them ten times better than all the magicians and astrologers that were in all his realm.

And Daniel continued even unto the first year of king Cyrus.

These were the men that God caused to be at the very centre of Babylonian affairs at the commencement of the succession of Empires that were to rule the world for a long time, while God Himself prepared to replace them with His Own Kingdom that will last forever. Their presence caused vital lessons to be learned, of which Daniel's book records several that today's men would do well to heed. The adventures of the four servants of God, although separate in themselves, are not to be isolated from the Visions or Prophecies of Daniel, for as History unfolds those Visions, it is clear that had the lessons learned by Nebuchadnezzar and Darius, or not learned by Belshazzar, been heeded, the world would be far more peaceful. One clear fact emerges, that heads of state, or governments of any kind, however powerful, can be brought to heel and disciplined or deposed by the Almighty, and they run that serious risk if they leave Him out of their calculations, and oppose His purposes. The Visions and

Prophecies of Daniel point us to the fact that the bigger these powers think themselves to be, the harder God will let them fall.

Chapter 2

2:1-3.   And in the second year of the reign of Nebuchadnezzar Nebuchadnezzar dreamed dreams, wherewith his spirit was troubled, and his sleep brake from him.

Then the king commanded to call the magicians, and the astrologers, and the sorcerers, and the Chaldeans, for to shew the king his dreams. So they came and stood before the king.

And the king said unto them, I have dreamed a dream, and my spirit was troubled to know the dream.

Nebuchadnezzar's First Dream: the king was troubled by the dream, and claims not to be able to remember its contents. One wonders why if he had forgotten it so quickly, it should worry him at all, or if he had some ulterior motive for saying that; perhaps he wanted to punish his wise men for misleading, deceiving or manipulating him about some previous unrecorded matter, which may account for his haste in ordering their destruction. It is evident from verse 9 that the king had some reason to distrust them, and he would not care too much for being told not to ask such questions of them. Although the dream had been lost, enough remained in his memory to make the king realise that it was first, important, and second he needed a higher order of help to understand it. We have to go with his statement that the content of the dream was at least mostly lost to him.

2:4-6.   Then spake the Chaldeans to the king in Syriack, O king, live for ever: tell thy servants the dream, and we will shew the interpretation.

The king answered and said to the Chaldeans, The thing is gone from me: if ye will not make known unto me the dream, and the interpretation thereof, ye shall be cut in pieces, and your houses shall be made a dunghill.

But if ye shew the dream, and the interpretation thereof, ye shall receive of me gifts and rewards and great honour: therefore shew me the dream, and the interpretation thereof.

It seems that the king was looking for confrontation with the wise men, he did not trust them, otherwise he would not have used threatening language in his opening remarks.

2:7-9.   They answered again and said, Let the king tell his servants the dream, and we will shew the interpretation of it.

The king answered and said, I know of certainty that ye would gain the time, because ye see the thing is gone from me.

But if ye will not make known unto me the dream, there is but one decree for you: for ye have prepared lying and corrupt words to speak before me, till the time be changed: therefore tell me the dream, and I shall know that ye can shew me the interpretation thereof.

Further confirmation of the king's lack of trust, he was telling them that they were a bunch of cheats and liars.

2:10-13.   The Chaldeans answered before the king, and said, There is not a man upon the earth that can shew the king's matter: therefore there is no king, lord, nor ruler, that asked such things at any magician, or astrologer, or Chaldean.

And it is a rare thing that the king requireth, and there is none other that can shew it before the king, except the gods, whose dwelling is not with flesh.

For this cause the king was angry and very furious, and commanded to destroy all the wise men of Babylon.

And the decree went forth that the wise men should be slain; and they sought Daniel and his fellows to be slain.

Daniel seemed surprised at the king's haste to destroy the wise men of Babylon. It is clear the order included him, so Arioch was giving Daniel a chance to escape, or intervene, knowing that he would not be involved in any previous dishonest matter.

2:14-18. Then Daniel answered with counsel and wisdom to Arioch the captain of the king's guard, which was gone forth to slay the wise men of Babylon:

He answered and said to Arioch the king's captain, Why is the decree so hasty from the king? Then Arioch made the thing known to Daniel.

Then Daniel went in, and desired of the king that he would give him time, and that he would shew the king the interpretation.

Then Daniel went to his house and made the thing known to Hananaiah, Mishael, and Azariah, his companions:

That they would desire mercies of the God of heaven concerning this secret; that Daniel and his fellows should not perish with the rest of the wise men of Babylon.

Daniel was trained to keep his head even if others were losing theirs, and gained audience with the king, and a day's stay of execution, because he confidently assured the king that God would reveal a matter of so great importance to him.

He then calls his three friends together to prayer, and during the night God gives him the same Dream or Vision the king had experienced, and its meaning. After giving thanks to God for the information Daniel returns to the palace and is ushered into the king's presence.

2:19-24. Then was the secret revealed unto Daniel in a night vision. Then Daniel blessed the God of heaven.

Daniel answered and said, Blessed be the name of God for ever and ever: for wisdom and might are his:

And he changeth the times and seasons: he removeth kings, and setteth up kings: he giveth wisdom unto the wise, and knowledge to them that know understanding:

He revealeth the deep and secret things: he knoweth what is in the darkness, and the light dwelleth with him.

I thank thee, and praise thee, O thou God of my fathers, who hast given me wisdom and might, and hast made known unto me now what we desired of thee: for thou hast now made known unto us the king's matter.

Therefore Daniel went unto Arioch, whom the king had ordained to destroy the wise men of Babylon: he went and said thus unto him; Destroy not the wise men of Babylon: bring me in before the king, and I will shew unto the king the interpretation.

The death sentence on the wise men would not now take place, thanks to Divine intervention.

2:25-30.   Then Arioch brought in Daniel before the king in haste, and said thus unto him, I have found a man of the captives of Judah, that will make known unto the king the interpretation.

The king answered and said to Daniel, whose name was Belteshazzar, Art thou able to make known unto me the dream which I have seen, and the interpretation thereof?

Daniel answered in the presence of the king, and said, The secret which the king hath demanded cannot the wise men, the astrologers, the magicians, and soothsayers, shew unto the king;

But there is a God in heaven that revealeth secrets, and maketh known to the king Nebuchadnezzar what shall be in the latter days. Thy dream, and the visions of thy head upon thy bed, are these;

As for thee, O king, thy thoughts came into thy mind upon thy bed, what should come to pass hereafter: and he that revealeth secrets maketh known to thee what shall come to pass.

But as for me, this secret is not revealed to me for any wisdom that I have more than any living, but for their sakes that shall make known the interpretation to the king, and that thou mightest know the thoughts of thy heart.

Daniel relates the Dream before the king. You can almost hear him muttering in the background, 'Ah, yes, I remember that now,' as each part is recalled. He must have been very impressed, and his trust of Daniel was growing by the second.

2:31-36. Thou, O king, sawest, and behold a great image. This great image, whose brightness was excellent, stood before thee; and the form thereof was terrible.

The image's head was of fine gold, his breast and his arms of silver, his belly and his thighs of brass,

His legs of iron, his feet part of iron and part of clay.

Thou sawest till that a stone was cut out without hands, which smote the image upon his feet that were of iron and clay, and brake them to pieces.

Then was the iron, the clay, the brass, the silver, and the gold, broken to pieces together, and became like the chaff of the summer threshingfloors; and the wind carried them away, that no place was found for them: and the stone that smote the image became a great mountain, and filled the whole earth.

This is the dream; and we will tell the interpretation thereof before the king.

Daniel now gives the meaning or interpretation of the dream. It is evident that in the Babylonian culture dreams and their supposed meanings as given by astrologers were taken very seriously. But this was in a class of its own.

2:37-39. Thou, O king, art a king of kings: for the God of heaven hath given thee a kingdom, power, and strength, and glory.

And wheresoever the children of men dwell, the beasts of the field and the fowls of the heaven hath he given into thine hand, and hath made thee ruler over them all. Thou art this head of gold.

And after thee shall arise another kingdom inferior to thee, and another third kingdom of brass, which shall bear rule over all the earth.

The Babylonian, the Persian, and thirdly the Greek Empires.

2:40-43.   And the fourth kingdom shall be strong as iron: forasmuch as iron breaketh in pieces and subdueth all things: and as iron that breaketh all these, shall it break in pieces and bruise.

And whereas thou sawest the feet and toes, part of potters' clay, and part of iron, the kingdom shall be divided; but there shall be in it of the strength of the iron, forasmuch as thou sawest the iron mixed with miry clay.

And as the toes of the feet were part iron, and part clay, so the kingdom shall be partly strong, and partly broken.

And whereas thou sawest iron mixed with miry clay, they shall mingle themselves with the seed of men: but they shall not cleave one to another, even as iron is not mixed with clay.

Fourth the Roman Empire. These four to rule the World until . . .

2:44-45.   And in the days of these kings shall the God of heaven set up a kingdom, which shall never be destroyed: and the kingdom shall not be left to other people, but it shall break in pieces and consume all these kingdoms, and it shall stand for ever.

Forasmuch as thou sawest that the stone was cut out of the mountain without hands, and that it brake in pieces the iron, the brass, the clay, the silver, and the gold; the great God hath made known to the king what shall come to pass hereafter: and the dream is certain, and the interpretation thereof sure.

Nebuchadnezzar is totally convinced.

2:46-49.   Then the king Nebuchadnezzar fell upon his face, and worshipped Daniel, and commanded that they should offer an oblation and sweet odours unto him.

The king answered unto Daniel, and said, Of a truth it is, that your God is a God of gods, and a Lord of kings, and a revealer of secrets, seeing thou couldest reveal this secret.

Then the king made Daniel a great man, and gave him many great gifts, and made him ruler over the whole province of Babylon, and chief of the governors over the wise men of Babylon.

Then Daniel requested of the king, and he set Shadrach, Meshach, and Abed-nego, over the affairs of the province of Babylon: but Daniel sat in the gate of the king.

Nebuchadnezzar is even more impressed. It must be unique for an Absolute Monarch to prostrate himself before his servant, and acknowledge his servant's God as supreme. He recognised that the God of Heaven had honoured him, by giving him great authority as the Emperor of Babylon, and by giving him knowledge far beyond normal human foresight. Nebuchadnezzar also was shown that his authority, and that of his successors was limited by God, and that his was a temporary order within the purposes of the God of Heaven that pre-existed his establishment.

He then promotes Daniel, to his 'Chief Executive Officer' and head of his Privy Council. So Daniel consolidates his position by requesting that his three friends who had assisted him by their prayers, be also promoted so that he would be more available to inform or advise his king.

We now have the strange situation of four godly men of Judah in charge of all Babylon. This pleased the king who knew that he had men he could trust near him; to use these men whose strange and foreign religion, exceptional knowledge, and the worship of their God, forbad them to cheat or lie to him was really novel. **It was revolutionary.** It did not go down too well with the worldly wise, and those who had become the rich, and the powerful by their devious manipulations of the king, and who now found themselves inferior to Jewish captives that they thought would have been better used as slaves.

The result of these changes would be far reaching, the black economy would be exposed, fraudulent returns to the Treasury would be detected, miscarriages of justice would have to be reversed, bribery would not be worth the risk of detection. Many lost the long held advantages of unfair practices.

The king would probably regard the detection of fraudulent returns to his Treasury as a priority, when he was informed of the true conditions in his kingdom. First it was time to overhaul the financial system. What would the king decide to do?

What are we to understand from this interpretation and what is its greatest legacy? After Babylon we have the Medo Persian, Greek and Roman empires, each symbolised by metals of lesser value but greater strength, the fourth being divided into two legs of iron terminating in feet and toes of mixed iron and clay. While the king saw satisfaction in being the head of gold, he was concerned about the future when he saw these inferior things a long way off. He also saw a Stone, cut by no human art, which struck the image on its feet causing the collapse of the whole structure to dust that blew away. The Stone only remaining to grow until it fills the whole earth. This Stone is not related to the other empires. It does not inherit its system from them, but direct from God Himself.

We are living at the time of the impact of that Stone on the weakest part of the image. Remember the words of Jesus, in *Matthew* 21:42-44, "The Stone which the builders rejected, the same is become the head of the corner:" "And whosoever shall fall on this Stone shall be broken: but on whomsoever it shall fall, it will grind him to powder." Jesus is here showing us that while Nebuchadnezzar was the primary king of the Babylonian order He is preparing to be King of His Kingdom that will replace all others.

Many accept the identity of the four empires from Babylon to Rome as those of *Daniel* 2, and can hardly say that they are not real, material and literal historic entities, but have great problems with the identity of the Stone Kingdom that God set up to run concurrently with them, becoming much greater and then replacing them, and what form it may take. (Some believe that because this Kingdom has something to do with God, it must be the Church or be in Heaven). But ask yourself why the Stone Kingdom should not also have a Monarchy, Laws and Territorial possessions since it supersedes the others?

It remains the responsibility of each of us to consider carefully its true identity and arrive as near as possible to the truth.

The Stone Kingdom: stone is a very durable material, our best buildings are made of it. It is therefore a suitable or apt symbolic material to describe that which God has long intended to do, and has been building while the four are running their allotted course.

God's message given through Moses was to Israel, "And ye shall be unto me a Kingdom of Priests, and a Holy Nation" *Exodus* 19:6.

David was made king "over all Israel and Judah" II *Samuel* 5:4-5.

"Solomon [son of David] sat on the Throne of the LORD . . . and all Israel obeyed him" I *Chronicles* 29:23. Like Nebuchadnezzar's throne and kingdom, these were real historic events that happened to real people, not some nebulous, spiritual or heavenly concept.

Further clarification of this is found in II *Samuel* 7:1-17 where the establishment of Israel's kings with David and Solomon is covenanted for ever, not by some bigheaded notion of their own, but by God's Word. Let those who think that they know where Israel is, and who they are, read these words again carefully, noting that they are to occupy another land, away from Palestine where this promise was made, and not be removed from it, and that they will have a Throne and hereditary Monarchy with David as ancestor. Furthermore the promises made to those who were concerned with Christ's birth, as in

Luke 1:27-35, make it plain that Jesus is destined to succeed to that same Throne within and over that same Nation.

If however we cannot find the Davidic Throne reigning over the nation of Israel, or at very least a recognisable part of it, we have a serious problem, and ignoring it is not a satisfactory solution for any Christian that believes Christ will return to judge and reign. We had better start looking for it before He returns. If it no longer exists, our Faith in God's Word is vanity.

This would be a very sad case: if God has failed to keep secure David's Dynasty and Throne reigning over Israel as promised, He is a failure, and so is Jesus who claims to be One with God. You cannot be certain of your salvation if Jesus' integrity is in doubt. We become as St Paul said in I *Corinthians* 15:19, ". . . we are of all men most miserable." We know that unbelief is sin, and brings errors in its train.

Every promise made by God has been, is being, or will be fully kept, and His Name will be found worthy of every honour.

The finding of this Throne and Nation should not be that difficult, with so many nations and countries becoming republics. There cannot be many left to choose from, and how many of them have Dynasties going back into deep antiquity? Remember this is the Throne of the LORD, with an earthly descendant of David as its occupant or custodian; it should be in a position where it will be at least fairly well known, and prominent in promoting the Christian Faith. Or, are we to believe that the God of all the earth has resorted to doing things in little dark corners?

In the past it would have been easy to make a mistake here. The Shah of Persia claimed the title 'King of kings,' and the Emperor of Ethiopia claimed to be the 'Lion of the Tribe of Judah': their thrones lasted a long time, but they do not qualify as contenders for they cannot now last forever, they have passed into oblivion. At the beginning of the twentieth century there were many thrones in Europe alone, but in that century the time came that he foresaw in *Daniel* 7:9. "I beheld until the thrones were cast down . . ." So God intended the other thrones to fall so that the Davidic Throne by remaining would be exposed and revealed. As Jesus said in *Matthew* 13:44, ". . . the kingdom of heaven [God's earthly - is on the earth] is like treasure hid in a field . . ." Like other treasures found in fields, it can be found by searching, as with a metal detector, or suddenly exposed for all to see by plough or bulldozer that destroys its hiding place. Jesus calls it the kingdom of heaven, because although on earth and earthly, he will cause it to function on heavenly, or God's, incorruptible principles.

In the end there are no serious contenders beyond the British Throne and Nation, and kindred peoples, that have done so much to propagate the Gospel at home and worldwide. Imperfectly, yes, but we always have been imperfect, the Mission of Jesus is to remedy all faults and imperfections and make us fit to be with Him. There is only one way to meet our Judge, it is with sins confessed and sins forgiven.

Chapter 3

3:1-7. Nebuchadnezzar the king made an image of gold, whose height was three score cubits, and the breadth thereof six cubits: he set it up in the plain of Dura, in the province of Babylon.

Then Nebuchadnezzar the king sent to gather the princes, the governors, and the captains, the judges, the treasurers, the counsellors, the sheriffs, and all the rulers of the provinces, to come to the dedication of the image which Nebuchadnezzar the king had set up.

Then the princes, the governors, and captains, the judges, the treasurers, the counsellors, the sheriffs, and all the rulers of the provinces, were gathered together unto the dedication of the image that Nebuchadnezzar the king had set up; and they stood before the image that Nebuchadnezzar had set up.

Then an herald cried aloud, To you it is commanded, O people, nations, and languages,

That at what time ye hear the sound of the cornet, flute, harp, sackbut, psaltery, dulcimer, and all kinds of musick, ye fall down and worship the golden image that Nebuchadnezzar the king hath set up:

And whoso falleth not down and worshippeth shall the same hour be cast into the midst of a burning fiery furnace.

Therefore at that time, when all the people heard the sound of the cornet, flute, harp, sackbut, psaltery, and all kinds of musick, all the people, the nations, and the languages, fell down and worshipped the golden image that Nebuchadnezzar the king had set up.

King Nebuchadnezzar had placed Daniel, Shradrach, Meshach and Abednego as his representatives and executive officers over all Babylon. The effect was dramatic; it led to the king overhauling the affairs of State, and in particular the financial system. This was because his new officers feared and worshipped God, and

His commandments did not allow them to lie, cheat or conceal the truth from the king. From them he learned of malpractices many of which had long been kept a secret and caused loss to his treasury. The king determined to put in place a system of finance that would be fully accountable to him, and at the same time control the lives of his entire realm. To this end, the king caused to be prepared and set up an image that represented Gold, possibly made of gold, but representing as a symbol the new use or role of Gold. The only detail we have is that it was ten times higher than its width, and its location; from this we may expect that he was introducing a decimal system of accounting. He was not representing himself as the head of gold from his dreams. The notion some have, that this was an image or statue of the king is flawed, no person is ten times higher than their width, a proportion of five to one might support that view. The procedure of worshipping the image was nothing new to Babylonians, it was part of their culture, so the king used established custom to introduce, and then enforce, his new system of monetary reform on his unsuspecting subjects. The dimensions of 60, 6 and 6 kinds of musical instruments are to return at a later date as they foreshadow 666 the number of the Beast of *Revelation*.

This would take some time to set up. It would require a system of supervision and period of training of the auditors, registration of businesses, and instruction in bookkeeping. A secure courier system for the transportation of collected revenues, and dispatching of royal commands and demands for money to pay for public works, would already exist.

Speculation you cry! Yes, but ask yourself what purpose the king would have in just creating a new religion? Babylon had plenty of them; it is not as if the king wanted to be worshipped, the image was not of himself. Nebuchadnezzar had better things in mind, he wanted to make a name for himself by upgrading the city of Babylon, by improving its fortifications, its palaces and amenities, to be the jewel of his empire. He needed lots of revenue, he was a big spender!

Officials of every Province and every strata of society were summoned to the Dedication Ceremony, This was a State Occasion probably with the army on parade as well, and in modern parlance it was the king, who with big show of power called the tunes, and when he did, they all reverenced the power he gave to the image of Gold. The use of various musical instruments is a symbol of the various new regulations introduced by royal proclamation, (not democratic process) and the assembly obeyed and worshipped the image, not from a religious point of view, but acceptance of the regulations, probably biting their tongues because of the pain in their wallets, but better than the alternative fiery furnace.

We do not know just what those new monetary regulations were, but the Bible indicates the Babylonian System as being inherited by the other empires of the series, down to Rome. On this assumption we can look at the present system, and make some reasonably close guesses or parallels.

1. All local currencies within the empire to be of a fixed rate or value to my standard wedge of Gold. This is an interim measure leading to a single currency in my empire.
2. All traders, businesses and professions to have their accounts audited by my registered accountants, for the assessment of tax to be paid in gold or approved merchandise to my treasury.
3. Failure to keep accurate accounts or to conceal income will lead to the seizure of all assets.
4. All loans will bear interest at the permitted rate, a proportion of which will be paid to my treasury.
5. All rates or taxes will be set by myself alone from time to time, as the needs of myself and the empire shall require, etc.

Its greatest legacy was a system of trading based on the supposed value of Gold. It stabilised values in the domestic economy. Any unit of any currency rated as being equal to a certain weight of Gold. It stabilised conditions for foreign trade. Today the Gold Standard is a thing of the past, and its passing has caused great misery and loss to millions the world over, and currencies are now influenced by the so called market forces, such that some have hardly any real value at all. Truly, Babylon today is in a very shaky condition after abandoning its Gold Standard. Throughout Bible Prophecy the name of Babylon is used to indicate these and other factors as they have been inherited by the whole of the succession of empires to this day.

3:8-13. Wherefore at that time certain Chaldeans came near, and accused the Jews.

They spake and said to the king Nebuchadnezzar, O king, live for ever.

Thou, O king, hast made a decree, that every man that shall hear the sound of the cornet, flute, harp, sackbut, psaltery, and dulcimer, and all kinds of musick, shall fall down and worship the golden image:

And whoso falleth not down and worshippeth, that he should be cast into the midst of a burning fiery furnace.

There are certain Jews whom thou hast set over the affairs of the province of Babylon, Shradrach, Meshach, and Abed-nego; these men, O king, have not regarded thee: they serve not thy gods, nor worship the golden image which thou hast set up.

Then Nebuchadnezzar in his rage and fury commanded to bring Shadrach, Meshach, and Abed-nego. Then they brought these men before the king.

Notice the subtlety. They knew, for they had taken special care to note, that these three were not at the latest ceremony at the golden column. So they put it to the king that these three thought themselves to be above the king's command. He had never questioned their loyalty, or thought he needed to, but he had to now. If he allowed any slur on his most trusted executives, he could see that all his plans would fall to dust. Bring them in!

3:14-18. Nebuchadnezzar spake and said unto them, Is it true, O Shadrach, Meshach, and Abed-nego, do not ye serve my gods, nor worship the golden image which I have set up?

Now if ye be ready that at what time ye hear the sound of the cornet, flute, harp, sackbut, psaltery, and dulcimer, and all kinds of musick, ye fall down and worship the image that I have made; well: but if ye worship not, ye shall be cast the same hour into the midst of a burning fiery furnace; and who is that God that shall deliver you out of my hands?

Shadrach, Meshach, and Abed-nego, answered and said to the king, O Nebuchadnezzar, we are not careful to answer thee in this matter.

If it be so, our God whom we serve is able to deliver us from the burning fiery furnace, and he will deliver us out of thy hand, O king.

But if not, be it known unto thee, O king, that we will not serve thy gods, nor worship the golden image that thou hast set up.

By the time they were brought in the king had time to reflect on the best way to deal with them. He thought a 'softly, softly,' approach might save both his honour, and his most trusted servants. Promise me that you will not fail to join in at the next ceremony, and we will say no more about it. This was a 'no win' situation; he knew that it was because these three men did only worship their own God that he could trust them so completely, and if forced to conform to Babylonian practices their merit would be gone. He hoped that by not making too much of it that the problem might go away.

Shadrach, Meshach and Abednego were not in a compromising mood. They plainly told the king that they would not conform to the worship of anything but their own God. What was worse, they claimed their God could rescue them, if it pleased Him to do so from the furnace and from the king's power. Now that is "dwelling under the Shadow of the Almighty" for real.

3:19-25. Then was Nebuchadnezzar full of fury, and the form of his visage was changed against Shadrach, Meshech, and Abed-nego: therefore he spake, and commanded that they should heat the furnace one seven times more than it was wont to be heated.

And he commanded the most mighty men that were in his army to bind Shadrach, Meshach, and Abed-nego, and to cast them into the burning fiery furnace.

Then these men were bound in their coats, their hosen, and their hats, and their other garments, and were cast into the midst of the burning fiery furnace.

Therefore because the king's commandment was urgent, and the furnace exceeding hot, the flame of the fire slew those men that took up Shadrach, Meshach, and Abed-nego.

And these three men, Shadrach, Meshach, and Abed-nego, fell down bound into the midst of the burning fiery furnace.

Then Nebuchadnezzar the king was astonied, and rose up in haste, and spake, and said unto his counsellors, Did not we cast three men bound into the midst of the fire? They answered and said unto the king, True, O king.

He answered and said, Lo, I see four men loose, walking in the midst of the fire, and they have no hurt; and the form of the fourth is like the Son of God.

All seemed lost to the king, there was no longer any room for him to show mercy, the benefits of his monetary reforms based on enforced honesty would be lost, he could only condemn the three to the furnace. And make it seven times hotter while you're about it!

They were arrested and bound by the strongest men, and when the furnace was heated to the king's satisfaction, they were thrown in. The excessive heat claimed the lives of the execution squad, they were the substitutes; three deaths were required by the king's order and three lives were spared by Divine intervention. The king from a safer distance in the grandstand, or rostrum prepared for the occasion, saw not three, but four men walking inside the fire, unharmed. Hurried consultation with officials, only three were thrown in. Looking a little closer he recognised the three, they looked normal, the fourth was outstanding, and he recognised Him as the Son of God. He remembered that they claimed that their God could rescue them; he thought it was just defiant words.

Their lives were spared, but at the price to the king of his three valiant men. Three men had to die, that was the decree, but God's principle of sacrifice of a substitute, in order to let the guilty go free, seems to be in operation here. The three soldiers paid the price of Nebuchanezzar's foolishness, so that he could witness God's Salvation.

3:26-27. Then Nebuchadnezzar came near to the mouth of the burning fiery furnace, and spake, and said, Shadrach, Meshach, and Abed-nego, ye servants of the most high God, come forth, and come hither. Then Shadrach, Meshach, and Abed-nego, came forth of the midst of the fire.

And the princes, governors, and captains, and the king's counsellors, being gathered together, saw these men, upon whose bodies the fire had no power, nor was an hair of their head singed, neither were their coats changed, nor the smell of fire had passed on them.

He knew he had made a gross error in his judgment, best try to put it right. He calls them by name and at the same time calls them the servants of the most high God, thus honouring the fourth person in the fire. The three stand before the king and his nobles who would not have missed the downfall of the three Jews for a fortune. Not even the smell of fire on them. They could have come from under a shady tree.

3:28-30. Then Nebuchadnezzar spake, and said, Blessed be the God of Shadrach, Meshach, and Abed-nego, who hath sent his angel, and delivered his servants that trusted in him, and have changed the king's word, and yielded their bodies, that they might not serve or worship any god, except their own God.

Therefore I make a decree, That every people, nation, and language, which speak anything amiss against the God of Shadrach, Meshach, and Abed-nego, shall be cut in pieces, and their houses made a dunghill: because there is no other God that can deliver after this sort.

Then the king promoted Shadrach, Meshach, and Abed-nego, in the province of Babylon.

So the king's plans were still valid after all, and his decree would discourage any similar plot to upset them, while publicly recognising the great power of the God of Shradrach, Meshach and Abednego. It must have been a very great shock for the king to realise that even as an absolute monarch, he did not have the last word, as he had previously supposed. Probably a greater shock for those who sought to destroy the Jews, and had come with joy in their hearts to witness their deaths, only to see them miraculously preserved, and honoured by the king, in front of all the notable persons in the realm. They feared revenge attacks on them.

It is an indication of the advanced state of Babylonian industry, to see the size of the fiery furnace as being large enough to allow four persons to walk about in it. Was it the furnace that was used to cast the image representing gold? in which case it would be capable of holding very many tons. Or was it the furnace used to cast the huge brass doors for the city's many gateways? How was it fuelled, and was it some form of blast furnace? Perhaps Archaeology will be able to answer this one day. Any bronze monument of sixty cubits high and six wide and presumably of say four from front to back, even if hollow would be a major challenge for any foundry today, and then there had to be the technology to move and stand it up. It would perhaps have been fabricated in several sections which would simplify the construction process. The Bible record only tells us what was made, not how.

Chapter 4

4:1-3.   Nebuchadnezzar the king, unto all people, nations, and languages, that dwell in all the earth; Peace be multiplied unto you.

I thought it good to shew the signs and wonders that the high God hath wrought toward me.

How great are his signs! and how mighty are his wonders! his kingdom is an everlasting kingdom, and his dominion is from generation to generation.

This proclamation is remarkable, it reflects the prosperity within his realm resulting from his firm stand against corruption, and that it was the wonder of God's power that enabled him to achieve this. He had discovered that the overruling power of God was to be respected. He was able to carry out many great works to improve his city, of which he was becoming very proud. It was this pride that was to be his next problem.

4:4-7.   I Nebuchadnezzar was at rest in mine house, and flourishing in my palace:

I saw a dream which made me afraid, and the thoughts upon my bed and the visions of my head troubled me.

Therefore made I a decree to bring in all the wise men of Babylon before me, that they might make known unto me the interpretation of the dream.

Then came in the magicians, the astrologers, the Chaldeans, and the soothsayers: and I told the dream before them; but they did not make known unto me the interpretation thereof.

The king's second dream cannot be understood and explained by the wise men. Daniel is not included in this although he is the highest ranking wise man, he does not fit into the magician or soothsayer schools but he never seeks to displace them or belittle them in the king's eyes, but waits until called.

4:8-18.   But at the last Daniel came in before me, whose name was Belteshazzar, according to the name of my god, and in whom is the spirit of the holy gods: and before him I told the dream, saying,

O Belteshazzar, master of the magicians, because I know that the spirit of the holy gods is in thee, and no secret troubleth thee, tell me the visions of my dream that I have seen, and the interpretation thereof.

Thus were the visions of mine head in my bed; I saw, and behold a tree in the midst of the earth, and the height thereof was great.

And the tree grew, and was strong, and the height thereof reached unto heaven, and the sight thereof to the end of all the earth:

The leaves thereof were fair, and the fruit thereof much, and in it was meat for all: the beasts of the field had shadow under it, and the fowls of the heaven dwelt in the boughs thereof, and all flesh was fed of it.

I saw in the visions of my head upon my bed, and, behold, a watcher and an holy one came down from heaven;

He cried aloud, and said thus, Hew down the tree, and cut off his branches, shake off his leaves, and scatter his fruit: let the beasts get away from under it, and the fowls from his branches:

Nevertheless leave the stump of his roots in the earth, even with a band of iron and brass, in the tender grass of the field; and let it be wet with the dew of heaven, and let his portion be with the beasts in the grass of the earth:

Let his heart be changed from man's, and let a beast's heart be given him; and let seven times pass over him.

This matter is by the decree of the watchers, and the demand by the word of the holy ones: to the intent that the living may know that the most High ruleth in the kingdom of men, and giveth it to whomsoever he will, and setteth up over it the basest of men.

This dream I king Nebuchadnezzar have seen. Now thou, O Belteshazzar, declare the interpretation thereof, forasmuch as all the wise men of my kingdom are not able to make known unto me the interpretation: but thou art able; for the spirit of the holy gods is in thee.

Nebuchadnezzar tells the dream to Daniel as a last resort when his other wise men failed, having then remembered that Daniel was good at that sort of thing. By the contents of verse 8, we could say he should have consulted Daniel first, and he knew it. At least his memory is now improved.

The king already understood the essence of the dream, that God gives the kingdoms of the earth to whom he pleases, this made Daniel's task much easier. It would otherwise be a very hard thing to find the right words with which to tell the king he was about to be removed from his throne, albeit only temporarily. Had his usual wise men said that, he would have assumed it was a plot, and an act of treason, simply on their past performance with his first dream.

However Nebuchadnezzar did see that at the end of the Babylonian succession their end would be brought about by base or unscrupulous leaders.

4:19-27.   Then Daniel, whose name was Belteshazzar, was astonied for one hour, and his thoughts troubled him. The king spake, and said, Belteshazzar, let not the dream, or the interpretation thereof, trouble thee. Belteshazzar answered and said, My lord, the dream be to them that hate thee, and the interpretation thereof to thine enemies.

The tree that thou sawest, which grew, and was strong, whose height reached unto the heaven, and the sight thereof to all the earth;

Whose leaves were fair, and the fruit thereof much, and in it was meat for all; under which the beasts of the field dwelt, and upon whose branches the fowls of the heaven had their habitation:

It is thou, O king, that art grown and become strong: for thy greatness is grown, and reacheth unto heaven, and thy dominion to the end of the earth.

And whereas the king saw a watcher and an holy one coming down from heaven, and saying, Hew the tree down and destroy it; yet leave the stump of the roots thereof in the earth, even with a band of iron and brass, in the tender grass of the field; and let it be wet with the dew of heaven, and let his portion be with the beasts of the field, till seven times pass over him;

This is the interpretation, O king, and this is the decree of the most High, which is come upon my lord the king:

That they shall drive thee from men, and thy dwelling shall be with the beasts of the field, and they shall make thee to eat grass as oxen, and they shall wet thee with the dew of heaven, and seven times shall pass over thee, till thou know that the most High ruleth in the kingdom of men, and giveth it to whomsoever he will.

And whereas they commanded to leave the stump of the tree roots; thy kingdom shall be sure unto thee, after that thou shalt have known that the heavens do rule.

Wherefore, O king, let my counsel be acceptable unto thee, and break off thy sins by righteousness, and thy iniquities by shewing mercy to the poor; if it may be a lengthening of thy tranquillity.

Daniel was shocked at the contents of the dream. The king realises that this is the hardest thing Daniel has ever had to do for him, and not to fear telling all. He explains the meaning of each detail of the dream, and its message. Finally, he offers advice that may, if heeded, by repentance and relaxing of his oppressive monetary policy to support his extravagant public works and lifestyle which had already reduced many to poverty, bring him God's mercy rather than judgment.

Would the king heed the warning, and mend his ways? He decided to press on with his programme of vast public works, higher walls to the city and all that, and to get the money to do it; after all he was the king, he would take the risk, he had a vision of a palace, and beautiful Babylon to complete, these must come first, as there was only about another year's work to do. He decided to continue with and finish his projects first, then afterwards there would be time to consider Daniel's advice.

4:28-30.   All this came upon the king Nebuchadnezzar.

At the end of twelve months he walked in the palace of the kingdom of Babylon.

The king spake, and said, Is not this great Babylon, that I have built for the house of the kingdom by the might of my power, and for the honour of my majesty?

He had just about finished his project, and was inspecting the final details. He was filled with pride and self satisfaction.

4:31-33.   While the word was in the king's mouth, there fell a voice from heaven, saying, O king Nebuchadnezzar, to thee it is spoken; The kingdom is departed from thee.

And they shall drive thee from men, and thy dwelling shall be with the beasts of the field: they shall make thee eat grass as oxen, and seven times shall pass over thee, until thou know that the most High ruleth in the kingdom of men, and giveth it to whomsoever he will.

The same hour was the thing fulfilled upon Nebuchadnezzar: and he was driven from men, and did eat grass as oxen, and his body was wet with the dew of heaven, till his hairs were grown like eagles' feathers, and his nails like birds' claws.

Nebuchadnezzar knew exactly what was going to happen. God had given him the dream, and Daniel had given him sound advice. His pride drove him on to complete his programme of public works. His problem as he saw it, was to finish the work before the dream became reality. Perhaps he increased his revenue to speed up the completion, thinking that he just might then have time to make some reforms to appease the gods. He took a gamble, but the odds are nil in your favour, if you gamble with the most High; he thought he had won, tomorrow would be soon enough to institute reforms to appease the gods; he could always consult Daniel about it. The work was completed in twelve months, and he inspected everything and found it pleased him. His pride knew no bounds and he claimed all the honour for himself. At that moment the Voice of Judgment came from Heaven, it is a rare thing for God to speak directly with a voice from heaven, and he knew he had run out of time. He had lost the gamble, and the kingdom too, it had not been worth the risk after all.

Seven Times (that is 7 x 360 days) living as an animal, he suffered for his pride. A day for a year of Israel's punishment as exiles. This may signify the fact that Nebuchadnezzar was the beginning of that period, and because like all men he was a sinner and his empire was temporarily (7 x 360 = 2520 years) to replace Israel's role, it was a sort of symbolic parallel with Israel's punishment by exile and future restoration, as he also was to be restored to his throne and all honour, at the end of his sentence.

It was understood by Nebuchadnezzar that the band of iron and brass represented both the period of his suspension (4 + 3 = 7 times, as the 4th and 3rd kingdoms of his first dream) and the security of the kingdom until the end of his suspension.

4:34-37. And at the end of the days I Nebuchadnezzar lifted up mine eyes unto heaven, and mine understanding returned unto me, and I blessed the most High, and I praised and honoured him that liveth for ever, whose dominion is an everlasting dominion, and his kingdom is from generation to generation:

And all the inhabitants of the earth are reputed as nothing: and he doeth according to his will in the army of heaven, and among the inhabitants of the earth: and none can stay his hand, or say unto him, What doest thou?

At the same time my reason returned unto me; and for the glory of my kingdom, mine honour and brightness returned unto me; and my

counsellors and my lords sought unto me; and I was established in my
kingdom, and excellent majesty was added unto me.

Now I Nebuchadnezzar praise and extol the honour of the King of heaven,
all whose works are truth, and his ways judgment: and those that walk in
pride he is able to abase.

God placed that mark upon him. It was a hard lesson to learn, but
he learned it well. In the same way the king's declaration of faith is a
mark or symbol of the enlightenment that will mark the return of
Christ, and the restoration of all the Israel kingdom under its glorious
King; and in a similar way the leaders of all nations will resort to his
wisdom.

One question remains, who ran the affairs of State during the
seven years of God's judgment on the king? We are not told this, but
who beside Daniel, and his three friends, whom none dared speak a
word against since the fiery furnace, and had been ordered to be in
charge of the Province of Babylon. They held all for the king, and
then handed it back in good order, to their restored and now wiser
king.

Isaiah 2:3.   And many people shall go and say, Come ye, and let us go up
to the mountain of the LORD, to the house of the God of Jacob; and he will
teach us of his ways, and we will walk in his paths: for out of Zion shall go
forth the law, and the word of the LORD from Jerusalem.

Chapter 5

5:1-4.   Belshazzar the king made a great feast to a thousand of his lords, and drank wine before the thousand.

Belshazzar, whiles he tasted the wine, commanded to bring the golden and silver vessels which his father Nebuchadnezzar had taken out of the temple which was in Jerusalem; that the king, and his princes, his wives, and his concubines, might drink therein.

Then they brought the golden vessels that were taken out of the temple of the house of God which was in Jerusalem; and the king, and his princes, his wives, and his concubines, drank in them.

They drank wine, and praised the gods of gold, and of silver, of brass, of iron, of wood, and of stone.

Some years have passed and Nebuchadnezzar's throne is occupied by Belshazzar his grandson. His grandfather worked hard to make his empire the best, and he learned some hard lessons in the process, chief of which is "that the God of Heaven rules over all."

Belshazzar inherited the Babylonian empire in a secure condition. and presumably grew up lacking nothing. He is remembered for his excessive extravagance, and such a desire to create a good impression, that his ego knew no bounds. There was nothing sacred, and nothing he could not have or do. Nothing anybody could do to stop him! What better way to demonstrate this than with a party to beat all parties.

This was some party, one thousand lords, with their ladies, his own wives and concubines, the chefs, waiters, and the wine waiters. The king size banqueting hall, with its kitchens and wine cellars was to be put to good use. This event would last several hours, with the need for cloak rooms and stables for their horses and grooms, all with attendants to provide for every need. Overnight accommodation would also be needed for guests from a distance.

The Medes were pretending to threaten the city, no chance of getting through or over those walls, but the land and river gates had to be closed at night; it was just harassment to cover up their real plans, but they would probably rob or kidnap wealthy travellers.

The king had welcomed his guests, and had a few drinks, perhaps he could not remember the new joke he wanted to tell, the alcohol was fogging his memory and he needed something really special to liven the party up a bit. He hit upon a brilliant plan. He would remind his guests that he was king in place of Nebuchadnezzar who had captured the golden vessels from Jerusalem's Temple. He would do a unique thing; he would let his guests drink from THEM. It is probable that there were enough vessels for each to have a suitable one; *Ezra* 1 mentions thousands. The wine waiters would keep busy topping up. This would keep the guests happy for some time, and toasts to the numerous gods honoured within the empire added purpose to the banquet.

5:5-8. In the same hour came forth fingers of a man's hand, and wrote over against the candlestick upon the plaister of the wall of the king's palace: and the king saw the part of the hand that wrote.

Then the king's countenance was changed, and his thoughts troubled him, so that the joints of his loins were loosed, and his knees smote one against another.

The king cried aloud to bring in the astrologers, the Chaldeans, and the soothsayers. And the king spake, and said to the wise men of Babylon, Whosoever shall read this writing, and shew me the interpretation thereof, shall be clothed with scarlet, and have a chain of gold about his neck, and shall be the third ruler in the kingdom.

Then came in all the king's wise men: but they could not read the writing, nor make known to the king the interpretation thereof.

The king saw the fingers write on his plastered wall. The candlestick may have also come from the Temple at Jerusalem, but there was no mention of it being taken to Babylon. In any case there were many candles to illuminate the large banqueting hall, and the fingers, and the writing. He trembled and shook in terror, and his wise men dared not attempt the task, and could not help him.

The Queen did not enjoy that sort of party but observed the unusual bustle as wise men were summoned by messengers, and knowing something was wrong entered the hall. From her knowledge of past events she was well informed, she may have been Nebuchadnezzar's widow, which would make her Belshazzar's grand or step grandmother. If she was Mrs Belshazzar, she was far wiser than her husband. She knew that this was a matter only Daniel could deal with. A runner is sent to summon him, and have him wait in the anti-chamber to the Banqueting hall.

In front of all those guests the reward had to be substantial. The offer of being the third in the kingdom, is simply that Belshazzar was jointly king with his father, they were therefore first and second, the highest position that could be on offer, was third. A footman would already have been sent to obtain a suitable robe and chain.

5:9-16.   Then was king Belshazzar greatly troubled, and his countenance was changed in him, and his lords were astonied.

Now the queen by reason of the words of the king and his lords came into the banquet house: and the queen spake and said, O king, live for ever: let not thy thoughts trouble thee, nor let thy countenance be changed:

There is a man in thy kingdom, in whom is the spirit of the holy gods; and in the days of thy father light and understanding and wisdom, like the wisdom of the gods, was found in him; whom the king Nebuchadnezzar thy father, the king, I say, thy father, made master of the magicians, astrologers, Chaldeans, and soothsayers;

Forasmuch as an excellent spirit, and knowledge, and understanding, interpreting of dreams, and shewing of hard sentences, and dissolving of doubts, were found in the same Daniel, whom the king named Belteshazzar: now let Daniel be called, and he will shew the interpretation.

Then was Daniel brought in before the king. And the king spake and said unto Daniel, Art thou that Daniel, which art of the children of the captivity of Judah, whom the king my father brought out of Jewry?

I have even heard of thee, that the spirit of the gods is in thee, and that light and understanding and excellent wisdom is found in thee.

And now the wise men, the astrologers, have been brought in before me, that they should read the writing, and make known unto me the interpretation thereof: but they could not shew the interpretation of the thing:

And I have heard of thee, that thou canst make interpretations, and dissolve doubts: now if thou canst read the writing, and make known to me the interpretation thereof, thou shalt be clothed with scarlet, and have a chain of gold about thy neck, and shalt be the third ruler in the kingdom.

So Daniel is brought in before the king who tries to make out that he always knew that Daniel could solve the mystery.

5:17-24. Then Daniel answered and said before the king, let thy gifts be to thyself, and give thy rewards to another; yet I will read the writing unto the king, and make known unto him the interpretation.

O thou king, the most high God gave Nebuchadnezzar thy father a kingdom, and majesty, and glory and honour:

And for the majesty that he gave him, all people, nations, and languages, trembled and feared before him: whom he would he slew; and whom he would he kept alive; and whom he would he set up; and whom he would he put down.

But when his heart was lifted up, and his mind hardened in pride, he was deposed from his kingly throne, and they took his glory from him:

And he was driven from the sons of men; and his heart was made like the beasts, and his dwelling was with the wild asses: they fed him with grass like oxen, and his body was wet with the dew of heaven; till he knew that the most high God ruled in the kingdom of men, and that he appointeth over it whomsoever he will.

And thou his son, O Belshazzar, hast not humbled thine heart, though thou knewest all this;

But hast lifted up thyself against the Lord of heaven; and have brought the vessels of his house before thee, and thou, and thy lords, thy wives, and thy concubines, have drunk wine in them; and thou hast praised the gods of silver, and gold, of brass, iron, wood, and stone, which see not, nor hear, nor know: and the God in whose hand thy breath is, and whose are all thy ways, hast thou not glorified:

Then was part of the hand sent from him; and this writing was written.

Daniel first states that he does not do that sort of thing for any reward or favour, but promised to explain the hand and writing. First he states why Nebuchadnezzar was so successful, he was appointed by the God of Heaven to rule that empire, and that he learned by bitter experience that He could take it away, and when he gave the glory to God, and only then, it was given back to him. There was a Royal Proclamation declaring this, therefore everybody knew about it, and there was no excuse for ignoring it. But Belshazzar did, he had learned nothing from the lessons of history. Worse, he used the gold vessels dedicated to the worship of the Almighty God of Heaven, and insulted Him by toasting his pagan gods whilst drinking from them. Therefore He sends you His message.

5:25-31. And this is the writing that was written, MENE, MENE, TEKEL, UPHARSIN.

This is the interpretation of the thing: MENE; God hath numbered thy kingdom, and finished it.

TEKEL; Thou art weighed in the balances, and art found wanting.

PERES; Thy kingdom is divided, and given to the Medes and Persians.

Then commanded Belshazzar, and they clothed Daniel with scarlet, and put a chain of gold about his neck, and made a proclamation concerning him, that he should be the third ruler in the kingdom.

In that night was Belshazzar king of the Chaldeans slain.

And Darius the Median took the kingdom, being about three score and two years old.

You have completed your days as king. You have not measured up to the standard required. All is to be given to the Medes and Persians.

As has been pointed out by Howard B Rand in *Study in Daniel* this message is primarily to Belshazzar, but further study shows it as relevant to the Babylonian System as a whole. The clue is the "weighed in the balances," for the words also fit Hebrew weights, and are equal to 2,520 gerahs, the smallest Hebrew weight. At one gerah a year, this shows us that the termination of Belshazzar was symbolic of the sudden demise of the Babylonian system at the end of its allotted time, as described in *Revelation* 18:1-6, with very little warning.

But Belshazzar kept his word in honouring Daniel, not that his special honour lasted more than a few hours. One might expect him to leave the king's presence feeling rather sick, and as his new office permitted, to instruct that the temple vessels be collected for safe keeping. Silently, while the feast was in progress, and under cover of darkness, the river that ran through the City, and provided it life, dried up. Darius' forces had dug a canal to divert the river, and they marched in under the boat barriers or gates, undetected, and entered the impregnable city, while Belshazzar feasted.

Chapter 6

6:1-3. It pleased Darius to set over the kingdom an hundred and twenty princes, which should be over the whole kingdom;

And over these three presidents; of whom Daniel was first: that the princes might give accounts unto them, and the king should have no damage.

Then this Daniel was preferred above the presidents and princes, because an excellent spirit was in him; and the king thought to set him over the whole realm.

Darius, a mature person, seems to have done his homework. Like many successful people he had learned from other's ideas and mistakes. He would remember the faithfulness of Daniel, who had acted as caretaker of Nebuchadnezzar's kingdom during his mental breakdown, and returned it intact to him on his recovery. The seven year indisposition of the Monarch is not going to be unnoticed in neighbouring kingdoms, or by ambitious nobles, and points would have been noticed as to how there might be a weakness to be exploited. He had his spies, and knew Daniel had been sidelined, and waited knowing that Belshazzar would be a gift for him to capture the prize of Babylon, and worked out a strategy. He follows the pattern of administration that worked so well in Nebuchadnezzar's day, and heads it up with Daniel. It is not mentioned that he was assisted by his three friends.

6:4-9. Then the presidents and princes sought to find occasion against Daniel concerning the kingdom, but they could find none occasion nor fault; forasmuch as he was faithful, neither was there any error or fault found in him.

Then said these men, We shall not find any occasion against this Daniel, except we find it against him concerning the law of his God.

Then these presidents and princes assembled together to the king, and said thus unto him, King Darius, live for ever.

All the presidents of the kingdom, the governors, and the princes, the counsellors, and the captains, have consulted together to establish a royal statute, and to make a firm decree, that whosoever shall ask a petition of any God or man for thirty days, save of thee, O king, shall be cast into the den of lions.

Now, O king, establish the decree, and sign the writing, that it be not changed, according to the law of the Medes and Persians, which altereth not.

Wherefore king Darius signed the writing and the decree.

There was resentment of Daniel's authority and that the king favoured giving him greater authority, probably because he would not tolerate any dishonesty, and even with careful scrutiny of his conduct they could find no reason or cause to complain to the king about him. There was just one chance if they could make him offend the king by his worship of Jehovah. It says something for Daniel's integrity if that was their only hope. They had searched Daniel's cupboards for skeletons and found none.

Today there is hardly a week goes by without some revelation concerning someone in high office; we should reflect upon why it is, that too few persons of integrity are elected or appointed in our administration. With the exception of Daniel it was at least as bad in the Persian system. They could not touch Daniel directly, but they could manipulate, flatter and deceive the king. They were right in their judgment that the king would fall for their flattery.

6:10-15. Now when Daniel knew that the writing was signed, he went into his house; and his windows being open in his chamber towards Jerusalem, he kneeled upon his knees three times a day, and prayed, and gave thanks before his God, as he did aforetime.

Then these men assembled, and found Daniel praying and making supplication before his God.

They then came near, and spake before the king concerning the king's decree; Hast thou not signed a decree, that every man that shall ask a petition of any God or man within thirty days, save of thee, O king, shall be cast into the den of lions? The king answered and said, The thing is true, according to the law of the Medes and Persians, which altereth not.

Then answered they and said before the king, That Daniel, which is of the children of the captivity of Judah, regardeth not thee, O king, nor the decree that thou hast signed, but maketh his petition three times a day.

Then the king, when he had heard these words, was sore displeased with himself, and set his heart on Daniel to deliver him: and he laboured till the going down of the sun to deliver him.

Then these men assembled unto the king, and said unto the king, Know, O king, that the law of the Medes and Persians is, That no decree nor statute which the king establisheth may be changed.

Daniel knew of the plot, but continued his daily devotions as before, knowing that he was being observed, and putting his trust in God. As soon as Darius knew against whom the accusation was made he knew also that he was deceived. He tried to find some device or legal loophole out of the dilemma, but could not.

6:16-17.   Then the king commanded, and they brought Daniel, and cast him into the den of lions. Now the king spake and said unto Daniel, Thy God whom thou servest continually, he will deliver thee.

And a stone was brought, and laid upon the mouth of the den; and the king sealed it with his own signet, and with the signet of his lords; that the purpose might not be changed concerning Daniel.

The sentence was carried out, but Darius made sure that his seal was included together with those of Daniel's accusers. He had expressed his confidence in the ability of Daniel's God to save him. He was making it clear that he placed no trust in his counsellors, and was making sure that there was no interference with the legal requirement, and no outside interfering or antagonising to excite the lions into a killing frenzy.

> *6:18-24.   Then the king went to his palace, and passed the night fasting: neither were instruments of musick brought before him: and his sleep went from him.*

> *Then the king arose very early in the morning, and went in haste unto the den of lions.*

> *And when he came to the den, he cried with a lamentable voice unto Daniel: and the king spake and said unto Daniel, O Daniel, servant of the living God, is thy God, whom thou servest continually, able to deliver thee from the lions?*

> *Then said Daniel unto the king. O king, live for ever.*

> *My God hath sent his angel, and hath shut the lions' mouths, that they have not hurt me: forasmuch as before him innocency was found in me; and also before thee, O king, have I done no hurt.*

> *Then was the king exceeding glad for him, and commanded that they should take Daniel up out of the den. So Daniel was taken up out of the den, and no manner of hurt was found upon him, because he believed in his God.*

> *And the king commanded, and they brought those men which had accused Daniel, and they cast them into the den of lions, them, their children, and their wives; and the lions had the mastery of them, and brake all their bones in pieces or ever they came at the bottom of the den.*

Darius went to his palace a broken man; he knew that if the lions killed Daniel, he and his whole kingdom would be dominated by a bunch of ruthless and dishonest lords, against whom he would be powerless. No wonder the dinner party was cancelled, no palace entertainment that night, and the palace plunged into silence. Darius would have sent his agents to keep him informed on any activity by

Daniel's accusers near the den, if possible he would be ready for their next move.

At first light the king went to the lion's den, checked the seals and called Daniel, and on getting a loyal greeting, joyfully summoned his guard to round up the accusers, their families, and to remove Daniel from the den. They all witnessed the breaking of the seals and Daniel emerged unharmed. Guards then threw the accusers to the lions who saw to it that Divine Justice was done. The Shadow of the Almighty had protected Daniel from the lions. The swift retribution on the accusers would have the effect of discouraging false accusers for some time.

6:25-28.   Then the king Darius wrote unto all the people, nations, and languages, that dwell in all the earth; Peace be multiplied unto you.

I make a decree, That in every dominion of my kingdom men tremble and fear before the God of Daniel: for he is the living God, and steadfast for ever, and his kingdom that which shall not be destroyed, and his dominion shall be even unto the end.

He delivereth and rescueth, and he worketh signs and wonders in heaven and in earth, who hath delivered Daniel from the power of the lions.

So this Daniel prospered in the reign of Darius, and in the reign of Cyrus the Persian.

Darius, upon the deliverance of Daniel, determined to ratify his victory over the deceivers, and to discourage any further plots against his trusted adviser. His proclamation declared that both Daniel and his God were to be honoured, because God had vindicated his faithful servant, and He had power to do wonders in heaven and earth. He thus recognised that he and his empire were in the hands of Daniel's God, and followed the pattern of Nebuchadnezzar by this proclamation.

To have witnessed those events must have had a profound effect at the Court of Darius, his sense of justice, and visible intolerance of corruption and deception would ensure a very high standard among his officials, with spin off benefits throughout his realm. That is not all; it has captured the imagination of millions throughout the centuries, and is still among the best known parts of the Bible. Daniel enjoyed the status of an honoured adviser for the remainder of Darius's reign.

Up to this point in the book of Daniel, we have seen his story as it relates to events in his lifetime, and how he was used to convey God's messages to kings. Those messages were in the first place for the kings, and were for their guidance or correction. At the same time the messages to the kings were also relevant to events over a long period, showing us that their lives were typical and symbolic of the series of empires, and the destiny of those empires within the purposes of God.

Daniel by his life of witness and work had an impact on both Babylonian and Persian affairs and he was much revered in life as well as death. Near the ruins of Susa in Iran (the Shushan of the book of *Esther*) there is to this day a Shrine in a good state of preservation that is claimed to be Daniel's Tomb.

Beyond this point, beginning with Chapter 7, we have Visions that Daniel was given, and they fall into a different class as they are intended to be understood towards the end of the period allotted to the four great empires first described in Chapter 2. For this reason Daniel was told to seal his visions, in a manner similar to the Seals of *Revelation*, only to be understood in God's good time. That time has now come, and those who diligently study God's Word and are prepared to take Him at His Word can find things that have been secret for centuries.

We have seen how the presence of these four men of God oversaw and influenced the beginning of the Babylonian series of Empires when He sent Judah into exile. How their legacy caused those Empires to develop in a manner of God's choice and foreknowledge, and how it was foreseen that it would at the end not be strong but ready to disintegrate.

In Daniel's day God made an end and a beginning. In a little while God will make another ending and beginning, but this time it will not be guided by four just men, it will be by the Power of Our Lord Himself. It will not be for a limited period, for His Work, that is, His Kingdom, as Darius declared, will last forever.

Chapter 7

7:1-6. In the first year of Belshazzar king of Babylon Daniel had a dream and visions of his head upon his bed: then he wrote the dream, and told the sum of the matters.

Daniel spake and said, I saw in my vision by night, and, behold, the four winds of the heaven strove upon the great sea.

And four great beasts came up from the sea, diverse one from another.

The first was like a lion, and had eagle's wings: I beheld till the wings thereof were plucked, and it was lifted up from the earth, and made stand upon the feet as a man, and a man's heart was given to it.

And behold another beast, a second, like to a bear, and it raised up itself on one side, and it had three ribs in the mouth of it between the teeth of it: and they said thus unto it, Arise, devour much flesh.

After this I beheld, and lo another, like a leopard, which had upon the back of it four wings of a fowl; the beast also had four heads; and dominion was given to it.

Daniel does not appear to be involved directly at Belshazzar's court until the last moments of his reign. He was still involved with God's Will, and was recording dreams and visions for our benefit.

7:7-8. After this I saw in the night visions, and behold a fourth beast, dreadful and terrible, and strong exceedingly; and it had great iron teeth: it devoured and brake in pieces, and stamped the residue with the feet of it: and it was diverse from all the beasts that were before it; and it had ten horns.

I considered the horns, and, behold, there came up among them another little horn, before whom there were three of the first horns plucked up by the roots: and, behold, in this horn were eyes like the eyes of man, and a mouth speaking great things.

It is easy to say that this Vision is a repeat of Nebuchadnezzar's first dream, using fabulous animals instead of metals. Despite similarities, if that was the case there would be little point in it as Daniel had already explained it in Chapter 2.

The fourth beast excites Daniel's attention more than the others, because its form and function changed from wanton destruction to verbal power as he watched.

7:9-14. I beheld till the thrones were cast down, and the Ancient of days did sit, whose garment was white as snow, and the hair of his head like the pure wool: his throne was like the fiery flame, and his wheels as burning fire.

A fiery stream issued and came forth from before him: thousand thousands ministered unto him, and ten thousand times ten thousand stood before him: and the judgment was set, and the books were opened.

I beheld then because of the voice of the great words which the horn spake: I beheld even till the beast was slain, and his body destroyed, and given to the burning flame.

As concerning the rest of the beasts, they had their dominion taken away: yet their lives were prolonged for a season and time.

I saw in the night visions, and, behold, one like the Son of man came with the clouds of heaven, and came to the Ancient of days, and they brought him near before him.

And there was given him dominion, and glory, and a kingdom, that all people, nations, and languages, should serve him: his dominion is an everlasting dominion, which shall not pass away, and his kingdom that which shall not be destroyed.

This is a new Vision, with new and different information, but covering the same period, and showing other forces that will be at work. A simple contrast is evident, in Chapter 2 the first, the head of gold is greatest, and the fourth although strong is the basest. In Chapter 7 the first is mild compared to the naked aggression and power of the fourth. Daniel sees the ignominious end of the fourth beast, followed by judgment and the rule of Christ.

This section ends with a near repetition of the statements or declarations of Nebuchadnezzar and Darius, concerning the omnipotence of God, and the certainty of the coming righteous kingdom.

7:15-18. I Daniel was grieved in my spirit in the midst of my body, and the visions of my head troubled me.

I came near unto one of them that stood by, and asked him the truth of all this. So he told me, and made me know the interpretation of the things.

These great beasts, which are four, are four kings, which shall arise out of the earth.

But the saints of the most High shall take the kingdom, and possess the kingdom for ever, even for ever and ever.

Daniel, who was gifted in the understanding of visions and dreams, is distressed to find this one beyond him. He asks to have it explained to him. He is told that the four beasts are not empires but kings. Obviously more than four individuals are required to cover so long a period as about two and a half millennia. They will have to be dynasties, or religious or political entities, or ideologies, etc. to be the motivating forces of those empires, with the emphasis on the FORCE. These are to continue until the saints are given the Everlasting Kingdom. This is not an adequate explanation for Daniel, who continues to enquire particularly about the fourth beast.

7:19-28.   Then I would know the truth of the fourth beast, which was diverse from all the others, exceeding dreadful, whose teeth were of iron, and his nails of brass; which devoured, brake in pieces, and stamped the residue with his feet;

And of the ten horns that were in the head, and of the other which came up, and before whom three fell; even of that horn that had eyes, and a mouth that spake very great things, whose look was more stout than his fellows.

I beheld, and the same horn made war with the saints, and prevailed against them.

Until the Ancient of days came, and judgment was given to the saints of the most High; and the time came that the saints possessed the kingdom.

Thus he said, The fourth beast shall be the fourth kingdom upon earth, which shall be diverse from all kingdoms, and shall devour the whole earth, and shall tread it down, and break it in pieces.

And the ten horns out of this kingdom are ten kings that shall arise: and another shall rise after them; and he shall be diverse from the first, and shall subdue three kings.

And he shall speak great words against the most High, and shall wear out the saints of the most High, and think to change times and laws: and they shall be given into his hand until a time and times and the dividing of time.

But the judgment shall sit, and they shall take away his dominion, to consume and to destroy it unto the end.

And the kingdom and dominion, and the greatness of the kingdom under the whole heaven, shall be given to the people of the saints of the most High, whose kingdom is an everlasting kingdom, and all dominions shall serve and obey him.

Hitherto is the end of the matter. As for me Daniel, my cogitations much troubled me, and my countenance changed in me: but I kept the matter in my heart.

It is this fourth beast that he was so concerned about, and for a very good reason. It had one particular horn, (a king, religious or political ideology) that harmed the saints, (the true faithful ones) and overcame them for a time until God rescued them. To have any understanding of this vision it is vital to establish the identity of both the fourth beast and the little horn. It will also help to see the significance of this by a comparison with *Revelation* Chapter 13, where a beast with ten horns, of which one in particular, is also described as having power to overcome the saints.

Revelation 13:1-10.   And I stood upon the sand of the sea, and saw a beast rise up out of the sea, having seven heads and ten horns, and upon his horns ten crowns, and upon his heads the name of blasphemy.

And the beast which I saw was like unto a leopard, and his feet were as the feet of a bear, and his mouth as the mouth of a lion: and the dragon gave him his power, and his seat, and great authority.

And I saw one of his heads as it were wounded to death; and his deadly wound was healed: and all the world wondered after the beast.

And they worshipped the dragon which gave power to the beast: and they worshipped the beast, saying. Who is like unto the beast? who is able to make war with him?

And there was given unto him a mouth speaking great things and blasphemies; and power was given unto him to continue forty and two months.

And he opened his mouth in blasphemy against God, to blaspheme his name, and his tabernacle, and them that dwell in heaven.

And it was given unto him to make war with the saints, and to overcome them: and power was given him over all kindreds, and tongues, and nations.

And all that dwell upon the earth shall worship him, whose names are not written in the book of life of the Lamb slain from the foundation of the world.

If any man have an ear, let him hear.

He that leadeth into captivity shall go into captivity: he that killeth with the sword must be killed with the sword. Here is the patience and the faith of the saints.

Same beast, same powers, but viewed at two periods, over six centuries apart, so some details will be seen with different perspective. It is best to use this method as Daniel had only limited understanding, because his vision was for a more distant time, but when John was writing *Revelation* the Roman Empire had come into being. Another important feature is the ability to change; this is a versatile beast, that is to say its motivating force can be kings, emperors, political, military, economic or religious, as best suits its purpose. It will also be noticed that in both cases blasphemy is seen. By the comparison of the two dreams, Chapter 2 and Chapter 7, it is clear that we are looking at the motivating force of the fourth or Roman Empire.

The winds cause turmoil in the sea (verse 2, symbolic for population masses in Scripture), it is the symbol showing that the political or other forces acting on the diverse populace of the empire, bring about changes often with violence. This 'Satan-friendly' Beast arises from and at its zenith, takes control of the massive and diverse population of most of Europe. How do we know it is 'Satan-friendly'? It makes war with the saints! Therefore whatever form it may take, if you love the Lord Jesus, beware, you have been warned. Much of *Revelation* concerns God's judgments of Babylon, and it should be remembered that Rome inherits Babylon's Charter, hence the Seven Trumpets, and Seven Vials of God's Wrath (*Revelation* chapters 8-9 & 15-16) fall upon Rome; firstly Pagan, then Papal. Their purpose is to discipline and give opportunities for repentance, and to demonstrate God's justice on behalf of the saints. Rome is forced to change because of this disciplinary action, so Pagan Rome gives way to become Papal Rome.

This is the horn that troubled Daniel because it had a man's eyes, a boastful mouth, and destroyed the saints. Little wonder his thoughts troubled him, he probably thought God's people had suffered enough by their deportations, some to Assyria and some to Babylon.

It is easy to see how the Roman Church became materialistic, and embraced idolatry, for when the British Christian Prince Constantine, who was proclaimed Emperor at York, eventually ended the Diocletian persecution, he put out of office all who opposed the Christian Faith. Those who wanted to hold on to their office, although Pagan at heart, became Christians, and by no longer opposing the Church held on to their power. Thus with the Emperor as its champion, and a massive influx of power hungry officials, it was impossible for the committed Christians to prevent the church being dominated by those who cared nothing for the finer points of their faith. The Church within Rome and the Empire became part of the State, and was controlled by it. Later with the rise of the Papacy the State became controlled by the Church; another change within the same Beast. Clearly a victory for this satanic beast which now controls a large part of the church, and then, as now, claims, despite plenty of historic and biblical evidence, to be the true and original church.

Daniel notices that the horn had the eyes and mouth of a man; it is not able to see as God sees, for it is blind to its own faults, and declares its own greatness and monopoly of truth, and that it alone speaks for God. Daniel also saw that the 'Beast State' was different from others, for it devoured the whole earth, treading and breaking. This was done first by military might, but in recent times it is economic power through the agency of international banking, and international companies that have caused the destruction of the earth's resources. Such is their power that for gain vast tracts of forest are being cut, the result of which will be massive mud slides, clogging and overflowing of rivers, devastation of towns and incalculable loss of life, and climate change, and none has the power to control these things. Truly the earth is being broken up to satisfy the appetite of this Beast.

Looking back at the earlier beasts, the second had in its mouth "three ribs," giving the impression of devouring, but Ferrar Fenton translates these as 'three tusks . . . among the teeth.' Those animals that have tusks can do you a lot of damage. These three forces will be at work and are used against the population at large by those who have achieved power. These are the basic forces of politics, economics and religion; they can be satanically inspired or manipulated. God intended mankind to have government, but He made it clear to Nebuchadnezzar, Belshazzar and Darius that certain standards were required, and that suitable censures would follow evil administration.

Yet another facet of this beast was observed by Daniel. He saw the horn wear out the saints and manipulate and change their laws, which of course would be God's Laws. By the 'Treaty of Rome' this is now in the process of happening. They blaspheme against God by declaring His Laws void. Daniel sees that the time allowed for them to do this is limited. The time period is given in the manner as at Nebuchadnezzar's suspension from his throne, and at Belshazzar's feast, but for only half of that period being 1,260 years, indicating the allotted time that God will permit the 'little horn' before its final judgment that will come suddenly. He sees it destroyed, but the other beasts, which may refer to the related forces of politics, economics and religion, now not dominated by the Papacy will last a little longer. This extension allowed them, may be required to prevent the nations from degenerating into anarchy, and to allow an orderly take-over by Christ. Then, the Everlasting Kingdom will be given to the saints, which is the Stone Kingdom seen as replacing all others in Nebuchadnezzar's first dream. Daniel saw the Christ coming in Glory to do that.

Chapter 8

8:1-4.   In the third year of the reign of king Belshazzar a vision appeared unto me, even unto me Daniel, after that which appeared unto me at the first.

And I saw in a vision; and it came to pass, when I saw, that I was at Shushan in the palace, which is in the province of Elam; and I saw in a vision, and I was by the river of Ulai.

Then I lifted up mine eyes, and saw, and, behold, there stood before the river a ram which had two horns: and the two horns were high; but one was higher than the other, and the higher came up last.

I saw the ram pushing westward, and northward, and southward; so that no beast might stand before him, neither was there any that could deliver out of his hand; but he did according to his will, and became great.

It is worth noting that as Daniel experienced this Vision, that it is in the form of moving pictures, as a film, video, DVD or theatrical presentation, similar to John's Revelation Vision; it is events taking place as he watches, and becomes personally involved.

8:5-14.   And as I was considering, behold, an he goat came from the west on the face of the whole earth, and touched not the ground: and the goat had a notable horn between his eyes.

And he came to the ram that had two horns, which I had seen standing before the river, and ran unto him in the fury of his power.

And I saw him come close unto the ram, and he was moved with choler against him, and smote the ram, and break his two horns: and there was no power in the ram to stand before him, but he cast him down to the ground, and stamped upon him: and there was none that could deliver the ram out of his hand.

Therefore the he goat waxed very great: and when he was strong, the great horn was broken; and for it came up four notable ones toward the four winds of heaven.

And out of one of them came forth a little horn, which waxed exceeding great, toward the south, and toward the east, and toward the pleasant land.

And it waxed great, even to the host of heaven; and it cast down some of the host and of the stars to the ground, and stamped upon them.

Yea, he magnified himself even to the prince of the host, and by him the daily sacrifice was taken away, and the place of his sanctuary was cast down.

And an host was given him against the daily sacrifice by reason of transgression, and it cast down the truth to the ground; and it practised, and prospered.

Then I heard one saint speaking, and another saint said unto that certain saint which spake, How long shall be the vision concerning the daily sacrifice, and the transgression of desolation, to give both the sanctuary and the host to be trodden under foot?

And he said unto me, Unto two thousand and three hundred days; then shall the sanctuary be cleansed.

This Vision of Daniel is concerned with the Medo-Persian and Greek Empires, and what developed from the latter. He lived to see its beginnings, but the time interval indicated in verse 14, 2,300 days (that is, years), brings us nearer to modern times. The Vision is an expanded view and a different perspective of the previous Vision of Chapter 7. The Ram represents Medo-Persia, the ram is a sheep, and indicates that it was an Empire including some of the dispersed ten lost Tribes of Israel. Cyrus was a notable king who was foreseen in *Isaiah* 44:28 & 45:1, and may have been a son of Queen Esther, hence his willingness to restore Jerusalem and the Temple.

Persian coins had a ram emblem on them. The Goat represented

Alexander the Great whose action assisted the Israelites to continue their migration. He also may have been of Israelite origin for Macedonians means Great Donians, implying a connection with the tribe of Dan. The single Horn of the goat may indicate a unicorn, also an Israel emblem in use to this day, Alexander certainly pushed the nations about. He also, on his way to defeat the Persians, paid his respects to the Jewish High Priest in a very peaceful manner because of a dream or vision he had. Macedonia and the goat connection goes back earlier to a happy incident when they followed some goats and found a new home, possibly mythical but the goat emblem was used on their coins. (See *Light from the Book of Daniel* by Augusta Cook.)

The emblems of these powers are confirmed by archaeological findings.

8:15-21.   And it came to pass, when I, even I Daniel, had seen the vision, and sought for the meaning, then, behold, there stood before me as the appearance of a man.

And I heard a man's voice between the banks of Ulai, which called, and said, Gabriel, make this man to understand the vision.

So he came near where I stood: and when he came, I was afraid, and fell upon my face: but he said unto me, Understand, O son of man: for at the time of the end shall be the vision.

Now as he was speaking with me, I was in a deep sleep on my face toward the ground: but he touched me, and set me upright.

And he said, Behold, I will make thee know what shall be in the last end of the indignation: for at the time appointed the end shall be.

The ram which thou sawest having two horns are the kings of Media and Persia.

And the rough goat is the king of Grecia: and the great horn that is between his eyes is the first king.

The two horns represent the Medo-Persian Empire of which Persia became the greater or higher part. The one horned goat is the Greek Empire as established by Alexander that conquered the Persians and became very powerful.

We have here a part of the symbolic representation or identification useful to us in understanding this and other prophetic writings; here we are told that 'horns' represent kings (or forms of national leadership). The Vision continues:

8:22-27.   Now that being broken, whereas four stood up for it, four kingdoms shall stand up out of the nation, but not in his power.

And in the latter time of their kingdom, when the transgressors are come to the full, a king of fierce countenance, and understanding dark sentences, shall stand up.

And his power shall be mighty, but not by his own power: he shall destroy wonderfully, and shall prosper, and practise, and shall destroy the mighty and the holy people.

And through his policy also he shall cause craft to prosper in his hand; and he shall magnify himself in his heart, and by peace shall destroy many: he shall also stand up against the Prince of princes; but he shall be broken without hand.

And the vision of the evening and the morning which was told is true: wherefore shut thou up the vision; for it shall be for many days.

And I Daniel fainted, and was sick certain days; afterward I rose up, and did the king's business; and I was astonished at the vision, but none understood it.

The unexpected death of Alexander caused a time of confusion in the Greek empire. Four generals took advantage of this and divided the empire into four, N. S. E. and W. as symbolised by the four winds of verse 8. From one of these now separate kingdoms, or territories, emerged a 'little horn' that became great in the South and East. This 'little horn' is not the same as that of Chapter 7 and *Revelation* 13 because it rises in an easterly location, yet the two have similarities, and may be regarded as being of a type, or pattern. This Eastern Horn sets the scene for the development of the Islamic Powers. Some have thought that Antiochus Epiphanes fulfilled this. He did desecrate the Temple by sacrificing a sow on the altar, and prevented the daily sacrifice, but he was defeated, the Temple cleansed and worship restored in 165 BC. He did not break down or destroy the Sanctuary, he only prevented its proper use for a time, and no way can Antiochus be regarded as 'great' among the empires in this drama. This explanation can only be at best a partial fulfilment because it ignores the chronological factor. We still need the identity of this 'little horn,' and to understand the chronology. We have to have a datum from which to calculate.

What are the biblically recorded events of Daniel's time that are concerned with the Sanctuary or Jerusalem? There are at least two of particular note:
1. The time of the removal from Jerusalem under Nebuchadnezzar, a beginning of the 2,520, seven times (7 x 360 years) of punishment of Israel, in this instance of Judah and Jerusalem in particular, (Israel's ten tribes had began their exile more than a century earlier) and Jerusalem being trodden down by Gentiles from 603 BC.
2. The Decree to allow the return of the Jews to Jerusalem and the Temple, 457 BC.

The first has had its fulfilment, and terminated with the capture in December 1917 of Jerusalem by General Allenby, without a shot being fired. Truly it was an act of God, and without parallel in the turbulent history of the City of Peace. Allenby was a Christian, and held the Commission of King George V, the then occupant of the Throne of David, from whom he was descended. Jerusalem was then, for the first time since Nebuchadnezzar took it, returned to a representative of the House of Israel. The Jews in Palestine who call themselves Israel, do not have a Monarchy, and are therefore not Israel in the biblical sense, even if the majority may think they are. (Remember, David's Dynasty was to reign over Israel perpetually, II *Samuel* 7 & *Psalm* 89:34-37.)

The latter is also concerned with the Seventy Weeks prophecy in the next chapter, of which more later. If however we use a little arithmetic, and add to 457 BC the 2,300 days (years) of the angel, we are at AD 1844. This date is significant. 1844-5 was the 1260th year in the Mohammedan calendar, from Mohammed's flight (AD 622 called the 'Hegira'), and that year is also 1,260 on their Lunar calendar from 603 BC. Therefore the Hegira is the midpoint between 603 BC and AD 1844.

This latter date marked a decline of Mohammedan power and the Turkish Empire because they were forced to agree the Edict of Religious Tolerance. Then if from the Hegira we move forward for a moment, to Daniel's final words in Chapter 12:12, 1,335 (lunar years) we arrive at AD 1917 when the Gentiles lost Jerusalem. Egypt's coins at that time had on them both dates, 1335 in Arabic type figures, and 1917. We have now a solution to the riddle of the numbers of days (years), and also the identity of this other 'horn' seen by Daniel, for it is none other than Mohammedan Islam and for some time represented by the Turkish Empire. The Eastern beginning and the breaking of its power are marked, together with the dates of the rise and fall of its control of Jerusalem, in God's Prophetic Word.

The condition in verse 23, 'in the latter time' places this 'horn' into the AD period, so ruling out Antiochus Epiphanes as a fulfilment of this prophecy, and the general description fits the Islamic faith that also enjoyed the support and power of the Turkish Empire.

There is a loose end to tie up at this point. In Chapter 12:11 relating to the daily sacrifice, we have the number 1290 days (years). From the time that Omar came to power, AD 634, that is he whose name is given to the Mosque on the Temple Site, it is 1290 years until the Caliphate ended in 1924, a further breaking of that power.

It was not possible to understand in Daniel's day, but the passing of time and the fulfilment of events has removed the seals from this formerly difficult and obscure Prophecy.

Chapter 9

9:1-3. In the first year of Darius the son of Ahasuerus, of the seed of the Medes, which was made king over the realm of the Chaldeans;

In the first year of his reign I Daniel understood by books the number of the years, whereof the word of the LORD came to Jeremiah the prophet, that he would accomplish seventy years in the desolations of Jerusalem.

And I set my face unto the Lord God, to seek by prayer and supplications, with fasting, and sackcloth, and ashes:

Shortly after the fall of Babylon to the Mede Darius, the son of Ahasuerus, Daniel was studying the writings of the Prophet Jeremiah. Some of what Jeremiah wrote was addressed to the captives in Babylon, his Chapter 29 is presumably what Daniel had on his mind. It is evident that Jeremiah and Daniel communicated, so that Daniel and Jeremiah kept each other informed privately, as well as in their official capacities at court.

Jeremiah 29:10-14. For thus saith the LORD, That after seventy years be accomplished at Babylon I will visit you, and perform my good word toward you, in causing you to return unto this place.

For I know the thoughts that I think toward you, saith the LORD, thoughts of peace, and not of evil, to give you an expected end.

Then shall ye call upon me, and ye shall go and pray unto me, and I will hearken unto you.

And ye shall seek me, and find me, when ye shall search for me with all your heart.

And I will be found of you, saith the LORD: and I will turn away your captivity, and I will gather you from all the nations, and from all the places whither I have driven you, saith the LORD; and I will bring you again into the place whence I caused you to be carried away captive.

See also Verses 4 - 9, preceding the above.

Please notice that God's message was to build houses, and live normal productive lives and not be led astray but to wait for seventy years, at which time God would begin the process of bringing about their return. It is also important to see that it was a condition that at that time they were to pray, then God would hear and act. It is therefore only those who kept the faith that would benefit from this promise, and this may account for the fact that after the 70 years of procreation only about 50,000 returned to Jerusalem. Many more must have remained in Babylonia. We must assume that there were many who had become so Babylonish that they either did not care or would not face up to the rigours of restoring Jerusalem. Daniel has therefore made this a matter for prayer. In order to better understand Daniel, we have looked at Jeremiah's letter to the captives. The remainder of the chapter relates to those still at Jerusalem between the first captivity that included Daniel, and the final destruction of Jerusalem some 19 years later when the Temple was ruined.

Judgment fell on Babylon not only Belshazzar, just 70 years after the fall of the Assyrian Empire. Cyrus, possibly prompted by Daniel, made his decree about the restoration of Jerusalem. Many returned to Jerusalem; but due probably to political reorganisation, which also unsettled the Jewish community, and local opposition the Temple was not rebuilt. It was at this time of political changes that Daniel would have searched, or instructed the archivist to find for him all the documents that related to the Jewish people. There would be many of importance, for instance those that related to the events and intrigues of Haman and Mordecai, that showed the separate status of the Jews within the Babylonian empire. He would not want any of these things to be lost to posterity together with the identity of his people, just because the Medes and Persians might think them unimportant. With this evidence, together with the word of God through *Isaiah* 44:28 & 45:1, Daniel had gone to Cyrus, and the first step leading to the return of some Jews to Jerusalem had been taken, and was put on permanent record, as a Royal Decree, that under the laws of the Medes and Persians could not be reversed.

On the one hand it may have been legal now for the Jews to return to Jerusalem, but they did not then seriously get on with restoring the Temple or City, on the other hand this Decree was binding on the State and there was the legal obligation to cause it to happen. It only required the political will to bring it about.

9:4-19. And I prayed unto the LORD my God, and made my confession, and said, O Lord, the great and dreadful God, keeping the covenant and mercy to them that love him, and to them that keep his commandments;

We have sinned, and have committed iniquity, and have done wickedly, and have rebelled, even by departing from thy precepts and from thy judgments:

Neither have we hearkened unto thy servants the prophets, which spake in thy name to our kings, our princes, and our fathers, and to all the people of the land.

O Lord, righteousness belongeth unto thee, but unto us confusion of faces, as at this day; to the men of Judah, and to the inhabitants of Jerusalem, and unto all Israel, that are near, and that are far off, through all the countries whither thou hast driven them, because of their trespass that they have trespassed against thee.

O Lord, to us belongeth confusion of face, to our kings, to our princes, and to our fathers, because we have sinned against thee.

To the Lord our God belong mercies and forgivenesses, though we have rebelled against him;

Neither have we obeyed the voice of the LORD our God, to walk in his laws, which he set before us by his servants the prophets.

Yea, all Israel have transgressed thy law, even by departing, that they might not obey thy voice; therefore the curse is poured upon us, and the oath that is written in the law of Moses the servant of God, because we have sinned against him.

And he hath confirmed his words, which he spake against us, and against our judges that judged us, by bringing upon us a great evil: for under the whole heaven hath not been done as hath been done upon Jerusalem.

As it is written in the law of Moses, all this evil is come upon us: yet made we not our prayer before the LORD our God, that we might turn from our iniquities, and understand thy truth.

Therefore hath the LORD watched upon the evil, and brought it upon us: for the LORD our God is righteous in all his works which he doeth: for we obeyed not his voice.

And now, O Lord our God, that hast brought thy people forth out of the land of Egypt with a mighty hand, and hast gotten thee renown, as at this day; we have sinned, we have done wickedly.

O Lord, according to all thy righteousness, I beseech thee, let thine anger and thy fury be turned away from thy city Jerusalem, thy holy mountain: because for our sins, and for the iniquities of our fathers, Jerusalem and thy people are become a reproach to all that are about us.

Now therefore, O our God, hear the prayer of thy servant, and his supplications, and cause thy face to shine upon thy sanctuary that is desolate, for the Lord's sake.

O my God, incline thine ear, and hear; open thine eyes, and behold our desolations, and the city that is called by thy name: for we do not present our supplications before thee for our righteousnesses, but for thy great mercies.

O Lord, hear; O Lord, forgive; O Lord, hearken and do; defer not, for thine own sake, O my God: for thy city and thy people are called by thy name.

As a man of prayer, there are few who can be a better role model for us than Daniel, and this prayer is much influenced by Solomon's prayer at the dedication of the Temple, II *Chronicles* 6 which relates to the exact situation Daniel was in.

His approach to the Almighty is in the tradition of his day, as a penitent seeking God's Mercy. He is uncompromising in his assertion of God's integrity, His faithfulness in keeping His Word, and of the justice in His punishment of sins, first on a personal level, and then at the national level. He confessed his sins, he probably felt contaminated by those things required of him in his official capacity. He must have been near to choking on the flattering words used to address the monarchs whose deeds he knew to their darkest detail.

He then catalogues and confesses the sins of the nation, for both those who were near, and also those in far off countries, and he was in a position to know where the supposed lost Tribes had gone. Daniel goes further by stating that the 'confusion of face' of his people is a direct result or consequence of their defiance of God, and totally their own fault; quite unlike the modern mind that finds it convenient to blame God and His imagined inability to prevent disasters. Then having made this comprehensive confession, he asks God's mercy and forgiveness and the restoration of His Holy City, Temple and People, as declared through His servant Jeremiah.

And then God gives him an answer to his prayer.

9:20-23. And whiles I was speaking, and praying, and confessing my sin and the sin of my people Israel, and presenting my supplications before the LORD my God for the holy mountain of my God;

Yea, whiles I was speaking in prayer, even the man Gabriel, whom I had seen in the vision at the beginning, being caused to fly swiftly, touched me about the time of the evening oblation.

And he informed me, and talked with me, and said, O Daniel, I am now come forth to give thee skill and understanding.

At the beginning of thy supplications the commandment came forth, and I am come to shew thee; for thou art greatly beloved: therefore understand the matter, and consider the vision.

While he did this the Lord immediately sent Gabriel to instruct and reveal how his prayer would be answered. He is told to understand and consider a new vision. This instruction seems to imply that there is much more information than first meets the eye, and this accounts for misunderstandings and misinterpretations that are commonplace to this vision. There is something special here, as Gabriel, one of the most high ranking angels, is not recorded as doing this with all visions, and is not mentioned as helping with the understanding of Nebuchadnezzar's two dreams. It seems that Gabriel telling Daniel to understand, empowered his understanding; and if we bear this in mind we may also be helped to understand.

9:24-27. Seventy weeks are determined upon thy people and upon thy holy city, to finish the transgression, and to make an end of sins, and to make reconciliation for iniquity, and to bring in everlasting righteousness, and to seal up the vision and prophecy, and to anoint the most Holy.

Know therefore and understand, that from the going forth of the commandment to restore and to build Jerusalem unto the Messiah the Prince shall be seven weeks, and threescore and two weeks: the street shall be built again, and the wall, even in troublous times.

And after threescore and two weeks shall Messiah be cut off, but not for himself: and the people of the prince that shall come shall destroy the city and the sanctuary; and the end thereof shall be with a flood, and unto the end of the war desolations are determined.

And he shall confirm the covenant with many for one week: and in the midst of the week he shall cause the sacrifice and oblation to cease, and for the overspreading of abominations he shall make it desolate, even until the consummation, and that determined shall be poured upon the desolate.

The 70 Weeks Prophecy has within it, and is comprised of, three shorter periods, these are: 7 weeks, 62 weeks and one final week. These, in the manner of prophetic time periods, are not weeks of 7 days, but represent weeks of 7 years, that is a year for a day.

With or without the final week this only brings us to the first century AD. Now that is fine, if we only consider the Jewish part of Israel in relation to the coming of the Messiah. To do this only is to stumble and fall, for failing to realise that this in common with much of prophecy concerns also the so-called Lost Tribes as well. Daniel, we have noted, had just prayed for those of Israel afar off in various countries, whose ancestors had been taken into captivity some hundred and thirty years before himself. We must consider this aspect also. How does this prayer for them get an answer? If it is not to be answered, say because it is contrary to the Will of God, why was Gabriel not honest enough to say, 'forget that, it won't happen'? Gabriel did not overlook this, but gave understanding of this Vision, and also said that some aspect of it was to be Sealed or not to be properly understood until a later period. Such Seals probably refer to the Work of Christ in opening Seals as in *Revelation*, which is concerned with events covering at least three millennia AD. Therefore we will need to look later for an even longer scale period than a 7 years week (or a day for a year) as the key to the sealed parts of this Vision.

Let us consider Gabriel's Message as it concerns the Messiah's First Advent, and the return of the Jews to Jerusalem, the rebuilding of the Temple and the City walls. The very nature of these Prophetic matters are inseparable from the time periods contained in them, therefore the correct starting and ending of these periods is vital to any understanding.

First things first, Daniel was enquiring into the 70 years predicted desolation of Jerusalem and the time of its restoration. He went into exile in 603 BC, at Nebuchadnezzar's first of three campaigns; the third was in 584-3 BC when the City and Temple were destroyed. By comparison with History, that is hindsight, we find this latter date is the relevant one as 70 years on is 513 BC, when Ezra commenced to build the Second Temple that was completed in 511 BC. The books of *Ezra* and *Nehemiah* record much local opposition to this work. The Decree of Artaxerxes authorising the continuation of the restoration of Jerusalem (that had run out of steam) was much later in 458-7 BC, when the troubles of the Jews were brought to the king's notice.

As a result of this Decree, the city was made secure. There is here a further point of interest. It will easily be seen that it was allowing time for the Decree to be served at Jerusalem and the work to be completed. It is a further 70 years from the commencement of the Temple before Jerusalem was finally put back in order. Thus was fulfilled the words of *Isaiah* 40:2, ". . . she hath received of the Lord's hand double for all her sins." Here let us also notice the equity of God's justice, for Babylon is also to receive "double for her sins" (*Revelation* 18). This, even if Daniel did not live to see it, is the answer to his Prayer.

Gabriel goes on to say, ". . . that from the going forth of the commandment to restore and build Jerusalem unto Messiah the Prince shall be 7 weeks and 3 score and 2 weeks; . . ." That is 69 weeks = 438 years. There were four Decrees:

> Cyrus (*Ezra* 1, 538 BC)
> Darius (*Ezra* 4, 520 BC)
> Artaxerxes (*Ezra* 7, 458-7 BC)
> Artaxerxes (*Nehemiah* 1, 445 BC)

Counting from the 3rd Decree of BC 458-7 forward, the 483 years brings us to AD 28, at which time Jesus was about 30 years old and was offering himself for Baptism at the beginning of His Ministry. The beginning of that period had been especially troubled for Nehemiah's men had to work with a tool in one hand and a weapon in the other.

The Jews also counted years in Jubilees of 49 years. From Ezra's mission in BC 513 that started the Temple the first Jubilee was 464-3 BC. By adding the full (70 weeks) 490 years we arrive again at AD 28. You will have now noticed that (70 weeks) 490 years is exactly 10 Jubilees. That means that it was 11 Jubilees, and the first year of the 12th from the beginning of the Temple to the beginning of Christ's Ministry. (It is not correct to detach and remove the 70th week, or part of it, to the end of this Age as is done by some.) The Jubilee was a year of release, it was therefore fitting that John the Baptist preached repentance, to introduce the Jubilee year, and for the introduction of the One that releases us from our sins.

This aspect of the Vision and Prophecy was to see the bringing about of several things, to do with the People and the Holy City.

1. To finish the transgression; Daniel saw that there were later troubles for the Jews, they ". . . denied the Holy One and the Just, . . . desired a murderer, . . . killed the Prince of Life, whom God raised" (*Acts* 3:14-15). Transgressions after that are not worth counting!
2. To make an end of sins; Jesus was Himself the complete sin offering, by faith in Him and His Sacrifice our sins are forgiven and washed away.
3. To make reconciliation for iniquity; "God was in Christ, reconciling the world unto himself" (II *Corinthians* 5:19).
4. To bring in everlasting righteousness; those that are in Christ already have this in God's eyes, but this will become a reality for all when Christ reigns on earth.
5. To seal up the Vision and Prophecy; those things that relate to the First Advent are seen to be fulfilled, or open for all to see. The details of the long range aspect remained sealed or obscured until they are applied to the greater part of Israel as it can be identified in these latter days.
6. To anoint the most Holy; the original words mean holy place rather than a person, and could refer to the Temple site. If this is thought of in the First Advent period, Jesus the Lord's Anointed did frequent that place, and cleansed the Sanctuary by removing the money changers, and saying, "My house is the house of prayer; but ye have made it a den of thieves" (*Luke* 19:46). On the other hand it refers to the Temple site where now stands a building and a form of worship that is inappropriate, presumably to be at some point removed. And the City of Jerusalem is to this day a turbulent and troubled place, rarely has it been the City of Peace that its name implies, its Peace has forsaken it.

We can now return to the 70 Weeks, and look at the even longer type of week. We saw that the period from the building of the Second Temple to the beginning of Christ's Ministry could be reckoned in Jubilees, as well as 7 year weeks, so what sort of period do we get from 70 times 7 x 7 years? That is 70 Jubilees, or 3,430 years. (We return to this in Chapter 11.) Remember Daniel was praying for and confessing the sins of not just the Jews but of Israel as a whole, all Twelve Tribes, the greater part of which went into captivity 130 years before Daniel, and here is the answer to that part of his prayer. The destiny of Israel as a whole and the Jews are shown in this Vision as linked in the Divine Plan, each having different, but vital parts to play.

In the 70th week on the shorter scale that started at Christ's Baptism, we saw previously that that event occurred at the end of 69 weeks of years from the Decree; this 70th period was also marked by the enlightenment of Christ's Ministry, at its beginning, but halfway through that period the Messiah was cut off, not for himself but for our Salvation and Redemption, also during the second half of that same seven years began persecutions for the followers of Christ, which have also continued beyond the end of that 70th 'week,' so we find that a similar confirming pattern occurs when we consider the longer as well as in the shorter scale of 'weeks.'

At this point it is suggested that those who wish more fully to understand the Angel's message should follow Daniel's example, not only of self examination before God as he did, but to consider also the state of the nation, as Daniel did and confess our collective sins, for it was only after doing this that Daniel was given a remarkable degree of insight to world and international matters as they impinged upon the future of all Israel. You too may know that you are greatly beloved of our Lord, may He give you wisdom and understanding.

Chapter 10

10:1-4. In the third year of Cyrus king of Persia a thing was revealed unto Daniel, whose name was called Belteshazzar; and the thing was true, but the time appointed was long: and he understood the thing, and had understanding of the vision.

In those days I Daniel was mourning three full weeks.

I ate no pleasant bread, neither came flesh nor wine in my mouth, neither did I anoint myself at all, till three whole weeks were fulfilled.

And in the four and twentieth day of the first month, as I was by the side of the great river, which is Hiddekel;

Daniel is explaining the time that he had received a remarkable Vision, the content of which was true and certain, but it was related to future events, some in the very distant future. He also states that he understood its meaning. He previously explains his concern for the future of his people. Now he has devoted himself to fasting and waiting on God for three weeks, and on the day of the Vision he was beside the river.

10:5-10. Then I lifted up mine eyes, and looked, and behold a certain man clothed in linen, whose loins were girded with fine gold of Uphaz:

His body also was like the beryl, and his face as the appearance of lightning, and his eyes as lamps of fire, and his arms and his feet like in colour to polished brass, and the voice of his words like the voice of a multitude.

And I Daniel alone saw the vision: for the men that were with me saw not the vision; but a great quaking fell upon them, so that they fled to hide themselves.

Therefore I was left alone, and saw this great vision, and there remained no strength in me: for my comeliness was turned in me into corruption, and I retained no strength.

Yet heard I the voice of his words: and when I heard the voice of his words, then was I in a deep sleep on my face, and my face toward the ground.

And, behold, an hand touched me, which set me upon my knees and upon the palms of my hands.

He became aware of a Presence, and looked up. Those with him were aware of a Presence too and departed in fear and haste. Daniel then describes the Person, the Angel of the Lord, that he saw, and it is very much like John's account of the Vision of Jesus he saw in *Revelation* 1, and the effect was to cause both men to fall down as when one faints. As he lay there unable to move he was able to hear what was said to him, then he was lifted on to all four.

10:11-17.   And he said unto me, O Daniel, a man greatly beloved, understand the words that I speak unto thee, and stand upright: for unto thee am I now sent. And when he had spoken this word unto me, I stood trembling.

Then said he unto me, Fear not, Daniel: for from the first day that thou didst set thine heart to understand, and to chasten thyself before thy God, thy words were heard, and I am come for thy words.

But the prince of the kingdom of Persia withstood me one and twenty days: but, lo, Michael, one of the chief princes, came to help me; and I remained there with the kings of Persia.

Now I am come to make thee understand what shall befall thy people in the latter days: for yet the vision is for many days.

And when he had spoken such words unto me, I set my face toward the ground, and I became dumb.

And, behold, one like the similitude of the sons of men touched my lips: then I opened my mouth, and spake, and said unto him that stood before me, O my lord, by the vision my sorrows are turned upon me, and I have retained no strength.

For how can the servant of this my lord talk with this my lord? for as for me, straightway there remained no strength in me, neither is there breath left in me.

This frail old man of ninety or so is helped trembling to his feet, and is assured of God's love for him, and that from the first day of his fast, it was God's intention to answer his Prayers. The Angel explains the reason for the delay of twenty-one days as being due to the opposition of the prince of Persia. This should be understood as an event in the spiritual struggle between God's Angels and the fallen angels of Satan. This struggle or war is every bit as real as the struggle between the material forces of good and evil; the Kingdom of God versus the Kingdom of Satan or Worldliness, that we see evidence of every day, and it is in parallel with that material struggle. The probable reason behind this delay was to do with persuading Cyrus (despite opposition in his Court that may well have been from the financial advisers' concern about the costs involved) to issue the decree concerning the rebuilding of the Temple at Jerusalem. The prince of Persia refers to the satanic angel whose 'duty' was to prevent, and cause officials to advise Cyrus against signing the Decree. The intervention of the Archangel Michael (who has responsibility to stand up for God's people having great power and authority) was there to secure the King's Decree at the exact time required in the Divine Programme for rebuilding the Temple after the first seventy years from the captivity, as recorded by Ezra in Chapter 1.

10:18-21. Then there came again and touched me one like the appearance of a man, and he strengthened me.

And said, O man greatly beloved, fear not: peace be unto thee, be strong, yea, be strong. And when he had spoken unto me, I was strengthened, and said, Let my lord speak; for thou hast strengthened me.

Then said he, Knowest thou wherefore I come unto thee? And now will I return to fight with the prince of Persia: and when I am gone forth, lo, the prince of Grecia shall come.

But I will shew thee that which is noted in the scripture of truth: and there is none that holdeth with me in these things, but Michael your prince.

In view of this High Power conflict being explained it is hardly surprising that Daniel felt unfit or unworthy to discuss such matters. It appears that Michael the Archangel was holding the situation at Cyrus' Court, while this first Angel answers Daniel's Prayers and instructs him with this Vision.

It is indicated in verse 21 that Scripture pre-existed. In the wonderful foreknowledge of God, there has existed a detailed schedule of events, and the duties that will be performed for God by His servants the angels, and prophets, and all those who put their trust in Him, together with the limitations that He puts on Satan's powers. This, before actually being revealed in selected parts to mankind through the prophets and written for our instruction, was always the Master plan from the beginning. God is not making the programme up as we go along; it has always existed complete from beginning to end.

Chapter 11

11:1-4.   Also I in the first year of Darius the Mede, I even I, stood to confirm and strengthen him.

And now I will shew thee the truth. Behold, there shall stand up yet three kings in Persia; and the fourth shall be far richer than they all: and by his strength through his riches he shall stir up all against the realm of Grecia.

And a mighty king shall stand up, that shall rule with great dominion, and do according to his will.

And when he shall stand up, his kingdom shall be broken, and shall be divided toward the four winds of heaven; and not to his posterity, nor according to his dominion which he ruled: for his kingdom shall be plucked up, even for others beside those.

We should note that the first year of Darius was the year Cyrus made his Decree. He outlived Darius seven years.

Although Daniel was told that the Vision concerned events in the distant future, the Angel puts it in context by describing first the near future. Daniel was not aware that the same angelic being had also assisted Darius, probably in persuading him to use Daniel the trusted servant of Nebuchadnezzar because of his integrity and wisdom.

The Angel first briefly reviews the end of the Persian Empire, the rise and fall of Alexander III of Macedonia, called 'the Great,' and the division of his Greek empire among his four Generals, as described in Chapter 8. In common with some other Prophecies, this Vision has more than one level or period of fulfilment, this is the first.

A total of four more kings are foretold for Persia, after Darius the Mede who captured Babylon. They are Cyrus and his son Cambyses, Darius Hystaspes, whose Decree caused the Temple building to continue, and Xerxes the Great who used wealth to wage war against Greece . . . but lost.

The mighty king is Alexander the Great, who did do what he liked, and nobody stopped him. He died unexpectedly while at Babylon, some believe he was poisoned and all he had gained was divided between four of his Generals, they each took charge of North, South, East, and Western parts of his Empire, as indicated by the 'four winds.' We now have kings of North, South, etc. controlling parts of the Greek Empire.

Alexander's embalmed corpse was paraded from Babylon in great pomp to arrive eventually in Egypt where he was laid to rest at Tanis, and he has been misnamed and misdated by several hundred years by Egyptologists who misread the Hieroglyphs.

11:5-6. And the king of the south shall be strong, and one of his princes; and he shall be strong above him, and shall have dominion; his dominion shall be a great dominion.

And in the end of years they shall join themselves together; for the king's daughter of the south shall come to the king of the north to make an agreement: but she shall not retain the power of the arm; neither shall he stand, nor his arm: but she shall be given up, and they that brought her, and he that begat her, and he that strengthened her in these times.

After the death of Alexander the Great, General Ptolemy Soter, first king of the South has Egypt, Libya, Palestine etc; the founder of the Ptolemy Dynasty. General Seleucus Nicator had North, being Syria to the Indus. He was the strongest of the four.

Soon Antiochus Theos gained the throne in Syria, and Ptolemy Philadelphus in Egypt, to avoid war in a dispute, (the Greek Empire being divided into four they all wanted more than just a quarter). Philadelphus forced Antiochus to remove his wife Laodice in favour of his sister Berenice, hoping to gain the Syrian throne through her heirs. This arrangement lasted until Ptolemy died when Antiochus removed Berenice and restored Laodice. That lady was not grateful, or of a forgiving nature, and poisoned her husband for dishonouring her. Then their son Seleucus Callinicus took the Syrian throne. They pursued with haste the fleeing Berenice, and killed her and those with her. They were all given up to death as prophesied.

> *11:7-9. But out of a branch of her roots shall one stand up in his estate, which shall come with an army, and shall enter into the fortress of the king of the north, and shall deal against them, and shall prevail:*

> *And shall also carry captives into Egypt their gods, with their princes, and with their precious vessels of silver and of gold; and he shall continue more years than the king of the north.*

> *So the king of the south shall come into his kingdom, and shall return into his own land.*

When Ptolemy Evergetes, Berenice's brother, found out what had happened, he went to teach Seleucus a lesson, defeated him and captured treasure and people and outlived him.

The 'Wig,' the constellation also sometimes called 'The Hair,' was so renamed in honour and memory of Berenice who had beautiful hair. This constellation was formerly and correctly known as 'Coma,' the Desired One. Thus a portion of the prophetic story in the stars was obscured and perverted.

> *11:10-13. But his sons shall be stirred up, and shall assemble a multitude of great forces: and one shall certainly come, and overflow, and pass through: then shall he return, and be stirred up, even to his fortress.*

> *And the king of the south shall be moved with choler, and shall come forth and fight with him, even with the king of the north: and he shall set forth a great multitude; but the multitude shall be given into his hand.*

> *And when he hath taken away the multitude, his heart shall be lifted up; and he shall cast down many ten thousands: but he shall not be strengthened by it.*

For the king of the north shall return, and shall set forth a multitude greater than the former, and shall certainly come after certain years with a great army and with much riches.

The sons of Seleucus included Antiochus the Great who attacked Egypt but was repelled and much of his army captured by the enraged Ptolemy Philopater. Antiochus later returned with an even greater army, and gained the victory.

11:14-19. And in those times there shall many stand up against the king of the south: also the robbers of thy people shall exalt themselves to establish the vision; but they shall fall.

So the king of the north shall come, and cast up a mount, and take the most fenced cities: and the arms of the south shall not withstand, neither his chosen people, neither shall there be any strength to withstand.

But he that cometh against him shall do according to his own will, and none shall stand before him: and he shall stand in the glorious land, which by his hand shall be consumed.

He shall also set his face to enter with the strength of his whole kingdom, and upright ones with him; thus shall he do: and he shall give him the daughter of women, corrupting her: but she shall not stand on his side, neither be for him.

After this he shall turn his face unto the isles, and shall take many: but a prince for his own behalf shall cause the reproach offered by him to cease; without his own reproach he shall cause it to turn upon him.

Then he shall turn his face toward the fort of his own land: but he shall stumble and fall, and not be found.

Some Jews thought to profit when they realised that the Vision indicated that Ptolemy Epiphanes would win the next war, but they caused Antiochus to regard them as enemies so that when he again controlled Palestine he destroyed many of them. The Romans favoured Ptolemy, so Antiochus thinking to gain time, and have himself in a better odour with the Romans, offered his daughter to Ptolemy, secretly instructing, or hoping, that she would betray him later, but she loved, or feared Ptolemy, and refused to betray him. Antiochus retired from his campaigns, and was soon killed when attempting to rob a temple, 188 BC. After Antiochus the power of Greece was superseded by the Roman Empire.

The Jews failed to learn from their rebellious mistake of trying to profit from, or help to bring about, or manipulate the fulfilment of Prophecy. After crucifying the Messiah they rebelled against the Romans and expected Messiah to come and rescue them from the crushing power of Rome. (The new king of the North for the time being, Egypt being king of the South.) They probably saw in Daniel's writings that God did intend to judge Rome, sometimes linked with Babylon, when Messiah comes, without understanding, as we with hindsight, that this would take place at a distant time, near His return.

Partial fulfilments of *Daniel* include Antiochus who desecrated the Temple by sacrificing a sow, and the Mohammedan powers who took and devastated the land and desecrated the Temple site with mosques. It is foolish to suppose that God has got to do a thing at a particular time, just because it would be very convenient for our plans.

We should give Him praise when we are able to see that He does exactly what He informs us about. If we allow Him to guide us, He may be gracious in allowing us to take some part in His purposes. We oppose Him and run the risk of His discipline if we attempt to force His hand.

To take a look at the long term aspect of this Prophecy and how it may describe events and conditions of our time, we need first to cast our minds back to the Seventy Weeks time scales that were discussed briefly previously in Chapter 9. It was noted that the Seventy Weeks as they applied to the period of Jewish history ending with Our Lord's Ministry could also be reckoned as Ten Jubilees.

We will now use this new scale of 70 x 7 x 7, or 70 x 49 years of Jubilees, that is 3,430 years, and apply it to Israel's nation generally in the Ten, or Twelve Tribes sense, instead of just the Jews, up to the time of Christ's Ministry. We should note that it was fairly immediately after exiting Egypt, that the nation was embroiled in warfare. Read *Exodus* 17:8-11.

We should see in this that their success or defeat depended on their reliance on their God; symbolically this was demonstrated by Moses holding up his hands toward God for Israel to have the advantage during the battle. They were at that time also being constituted into a Nation, with Laws under God, that included the observance of Jubilees, taught and administered by Moses; whereas previously they were a collection of Tribes or Clans lacking cohesive leadership.

In the long term therefore we can say that Israel's warfare began in Moses' time. Gabriel stated, ". . . unto the end of the war desolations are determined" (*Daniel* 9:26). If the coming and mission of Messiah was accomplished in seventy weeks of years, may not the warfare of Israel, as God's "new sharp threshing instrument" (*Isaiah* 41:15) be completed in seventy Jubilees?

If the first Jubilee began 1488-7 BC, and 70 Jubilees or 3430 years on we arrive at AD 1944. Most will recognise immediately that World War II was then drawing to a close after Days of Prayer for Divine help. This may show us the period and conclusion of Israel's warfare, during which time Israel has been used of God to correct, discipline or break aggressive nations or ideologies; not only so but with the important Divine Promise. Read *Isaiah* 54:17.

(The terms, 'king of the north, ... south,' are relative terms, applied to other nations as they do occur within the Daniel Vision.) It is evident from history that Britain and USA, the most easily recognised parts of Israel under the New Covenant, that is nominally Christian, have had many wars for several centuries, without suffering defeat, up to the end of World War II. From what has just been read we can see why, despite that promise, there were sometimes heavy losses, and as Moses soon saw it needed a concerted effort together with continual reliance on God to secure the desired outcome. Many can remember that was the case on a number of other occasions, including Dunkirk, when there were National Days of Prayer.

Since 1945 the USA has had military disasters and humiliations, of which Vietnam is among its most painful memories. Britain and the Commonwealth too have suffered at the hands of terrorists, who cause disruption and severe loss, against whom we seem powerless, and have resorted to appeasement with predictable results. We have embarked on so-called peace keeping missions, and this causes even greater suffering and increases the numbers of refugees who are an intolerable burden both in expense and accommodation. But what is the alternative? There may not be one yet! For, as the rise from obscurity of the modern Israel nations to great power was predicted, so too is their decline. The Angel stated in Chapter 12:8, ". . . to scatter the power of the holy people," (Israel in its Christian form under the New Covenant). **We are currently losing reliance on God and our power diminishes in that proportion, and that is a marker of where we are in Prophetic Time.**

As a means of showing the ways in which this angelic message has been both explained and also concealed, each verse or group of verses indicates either a partial or complete fulfilling of events in the past, or future. This is but a rough guide, and the reader is invited to look even more closely, as the discernment of this message is only for the faithful who like Daniel seek the Holy Spirit's help.

11:20. Then shall stand up in his estate a raiser of taxes in the glory of the kingdom: but within few days he shall be destroyed, neither in anger, nor in battle.

Antiochus, being hard up, retired from his campaigns and was soon killed when attempting to rob a temple, 188 BC.

11:24-27. He shall enter peaceably even upon the fattest places of the province; and he shall do that which his fathers have not done, nor his fathers' fathers; he shall scatter among them the prey, and spoil, and riches: yea, and he shall forecast his devices against the strongholds, even for a time.

And he shall stir up his power and his courage against the king of the south with a great army; and the king of the south shall be stirred up to battle with a very great and mighty army; but he shall not stand: for they shall forecast devices against him.

Yea, they that feed of the portion of his meat shall destroy him, and his army shall overflow: and many shall fall down slain.

And both these kings' hearts shall be to do mischief, and they shall speak lies at one table; but it shall not prosper: for yet the end shall be at the time appointed.

We are obviously looking at a different 'he.' Such is the compression factor of this message that small clues are vital for identifying persons or nations, or to separate the nearer from the more distant meanings.

11:28-31. Then shall he return into his land with great riches; and his heart shall be against the holy covenant; and he shall do exploits, and return to his own land.

At the time appointed he shall return, and come toward the south; but it shall not be as the former, or the latter.

For the ships of Chittim shall come against him: therefore he shall be grieved, and return, and have indignation against the holy covenant: so shall he do; he shall even return, and have intelligence with them that forsake the holy covenant.

And arms shall stand on his part, and they shall pollute the sanctuary of strength, and shall take away the daily sacrifice, and they shall place the abomination that maketh desolate.

Sadly the Jews seem not to have learned the lessons from history, but suppose that they may take as a God given right, Jerusalem and the land by force, regardless of the fact that they place themselves outside of God's favour by continuing to deny His Messiah. Jewry, or

Zionism, is very busy setting up a One World Government by their control of Banking, and exploiting the notion that they are God's Chosen People. The Christian Churches, through disregard of Scripture seem to support this view, in spite of their Lord's words to the contrary. See *Matthew* 21:33-46 and take special note of verses 43 & 45. We have yet to see the full disastrous consequences of this folly, but the way events and confrontation policies are now shaping Palestine we may not have long to wait. Thus we see that this section of Daniel's Vision and Prophecy has had at least three, and may yet be four levels or phases of fulfilment. (Some do suppose that the final or seventieth week is detached from the other sixty-nine, and will occur at the end of this age, thereby creating a gap or vacuum in God's timekeeping and are still looking for an event by which they can determine its beginning, sadly they are looking for a present or future event that is now past.)

This is probably the most important factor in the Sealing and understanding of Daniel, until the crisis in these last days, for many have followed the earlier fulfilment, without accepting as serious the Angel's advice to note that it concerned also the crisis at the end of the times. (Meaning the 'Times of the Gentiles,' or the end of 'Seven Times' of Israel's chastisement.)

11:32-35.   And such as do wickedly against the covenant shall he corrupt by flatteries: but the people that do know their God shall be strong, and do exploits.

And they that understand among the people shall instruct many: yet they shall fall by the sword, and by flame, by captivity, and by spoil, many days.

Now when they shall fall, they shall be holpen with a little help: but many shall cleave to them with flatteries.

And some of them of understanding shall fall, to try them, and to purge, and to make them white, even to the time of the end: because it is yet for a time appointed.

This is a description or outline of the persecutions of the early Church, by and within the Pagan Roman Empire, continuing into the Holy Roman Empire, and shows the deprivations and tortures endured by those who professed that Jesus Christ was their Lord.

This passage follows the description of the destruction of Jerusalem and the Desolation symbolised by the Mosque of Omar on the Temple site. AD 637. In a few years the Pope Theodorus I claimed to be the Sovereign Pontiff, and Pope Vitalian AD 657-672, required the use of only Latin in Divine Worship, just 666 (Beast Number) years from the birth of Christ! This seems to be the beginning of fanatical religious persecutions. The statement that "many shall fall by the sword and by flame, by captivity, and by spoil, many days" is a fair description of the Dark Middle Ages; but this period may not be fully ended yet, it may also repeat in another context. Those of understanding might still face trials, and be purified as they oppose Rome's (Babylon's) errors, as is currently occurring in the New World, until the appointed time. In *Revelation* this is referred to as the Two Witnesses in sackcloth.

11:36-39. And the king shall do according to his will; and he shall exalt himself, and magnify himself above every god, and shall speak marvellous things against the God of gods, and shall prosper till the indignation be accomplished: for that that is determined shall be done.

Neither shall he regard the God of his fathers, nor the desire of women, nor regard any god: for he shall magnify himself above all.

But in his estate shall he honour the God of forces: and a god whom his fathers knew not shall he honour with gold, and silver, and with precious stones, and pleasant things.

Thus shall he do in the most strong holds with a strange god, whom he shall acknowledge and increase with glory: and he shall cause them to rule over many, and shall divide the land for gain.

This shows the development of Rome from being a Military Empire to the Papacy that claims that it has jurisdiction over the whole world, thus placing it in its own eyes as being above Christ. With regard also to Islam, the features of force and degrading women and denial of the True God also fit.

The true Christian Faith had been established despite persecution in Rome as in many other towns and districts by the Apostles. Rome invented its own form of Faith that includes some earlier pagan elements, such as the worship of mother and child, and disregarded the teachings of the Apostles. This they promoted with great vigour, claiming it to be the only true faith and used force or torture equal to that used by Pagan Rome against all who count Jesus of Nazareth to be Christ the Only Saviour and Lord of All.

It should be remembered that the title of king as used in Daniel equals a national or ideological leader as a president or dictator, like the use of prince earlier in this study. This type is so full of arrogance as to feel under no obligation to God, or any established authority or tradition, and to have an unnatural attitude to women. As we shall see there is a series of partial fulfilments, ending with a complete fulfilment of this type.

These two verses describe in a very few words the character of the Roman Catholic Church, and the policy of the Popes in particular. The use of force and execution of any who dare to oppose their teaching or authority. This authority is maintained where possible by force or coercion and by distortion of the Gospel of Jesus, making Salvation only obtainable through obedience to their Church, rather than the free gift of God by Repentance and Faith. They also forbid the Priests to marry which the Bible allows. The God of Force is honoured, but the early Church Fathers rejected force or the accumulation of material power or riches. This is also described in *Revelation* 6 in the 5th Seal.

> *11:40-45. And at the time of the end shall the king of the south push at him: and the king of the north shall come against him like a whirlwind, with chariots, and with horsemen, and with many ships; and he shall enter into the countries, and shall overflow and pass over.*

He shall enter also into the glorious land, and many countries shall be overthrown: but these shall escape out of his hand, even Edom, and Moab, and the chief of the children of Ammon.

He shall stretch forth his hand also upon the countries: and the land of Egypt shall not escape.

But he shall have power over the treasures of gold and of silver, and over all the precious things of Egypt: and the Libyans and the Ethiopians shall be at his steps.

But tidings out of the east and out of the north shall trouble him: therefore he shall go forth with great fury to destroy, and utterly to make away many.

And he shall plant the tabernacles of his palace between the seas in the glorious holy mountain; yet he shall come to his end, and none shall help him.

Let us move forward to the rise of Germany as the leading nation of Europe. Power had come to them from the successors of the Roman Empire, via Rome, the Papacy and France. And World War I comes just 2,520 years after the rise of Nebuchadnezzar when at the end of 1917 the British gained control of Jerusalem, which ended the times of the Gentiles and set the scene for new developments. We now in particular look at the rise of Adolf Hitler. Germany in common with many countries suffered from depression and more than most from rampant inflation between World War I and World War II. Some think that Hitler blamed the Jews for this, and even if that is correct it is never an excuse to commit atrocities. Powers that were not given to him he seized, declaring that he would make Germany great. He had popular support, and in the context of rampant inflation any new approach to power and politics looked a good thing, clearly something did have to be done, and Hitler said he was the man for the job. We should regard Hitler as the 'him' mentioned twice in verse 40.

Let us compare Hitler and Germany and the events of his day with the Prophecy, at the same time we can note the similarity between his and Napoleon's campaigns. Hitler like Napoleon used the resources of the nation to generate powerful armed services, and his campaigns were likewise successful, in Europe and the African continent. In World War I Germany was active in Palestine, providing intelligence and military aircraft for the Turkish Forces, and General Allenby for that reason was determined to keep their aircraft out of the skies. Palestine was a detail that escaped Napoleon's attention. Hitler visualised a German Empire that he would obtain by force of arms to equal, and of course supplant the British Empire. Inevitably his exploits brought him into conflict with Britain, whom he also like Napoleon prepared to invade. When the invasion plans were prepared like Napoleon, Hitler after all the damage done in the Battle of Britain suddenly turned his attention to Russia. Like Napoleon before him, his timing was disastrous, for the severe Russian winter caused insurmountable problems for his troops, so that he then had tidings of the Russian advance from the East and North. In 1945 his defeat was on cue at just 70 Jubilees from the Exodus, thus completing the period when Russia, like Cyrus, became God's 'Battle Axe' of *Jeremiah* 51:20. Thus came near to its end the series of powers starting with Babylon. The description of this conflict is of interest, in that Russia made it a race to reach Berlin, and almost before anyone could draw breath had overflowed into and gained control of several East European countries, the use of aircraft is implied by passing over. It is a fact that Russia destroyed some 80 per cent of the Nazi Germany forces of military 'Babylon' in the European 'Armageddon' scene. The hammer and sickle emblem symbolised the cutting down at the harvest while the hammer, or maul, the 'battle axe' to break in pieces a dominant and openly arrogant 'beast' power driven by one of the unclean spirits of *Revelation* 16:13-16.

We are now awaiting the culmination of events, so that we are not now looking at the Prophetic Word in hindsight, and comparing it with established history. Let us be like Daniel and seek the Lord's favour and guidance from His Spirit of Truth.

"Lord Jesus, we have been looking at the wonders of your foreknowledge as revealed in this Vision that you gave to Daniel, and like him we desire to know more. We ask that your Holy Spirit will give us understanding, and make us a people prepared for your service in the days to come. Amen."

The end of the Cold War and the reunification of Germany in 1990 in effect completed the process of the drying up of the prophetic Euphrates to allow the further advance of Russia westward to confront the European Union which at any moment could implode – particularly as a result of the break-up of the eurozone.

The sudden eruption of the crisis in the Ukraine in November 2013 and the Russian movement of its forces in the Crimean region threaten to spread westward into the territory of the European Union. The final debacle may be near in which Germany moves east again to accommodate Russia and further disruption in the Ukraine and the Balkans.

Events are moving very fast as we write and a second Crimean War begins to look possible coming 160 years exactly from the nineteenth century conflict (October 1853 – February 1856). This is one-tenth of the Battle Line number of 1600 found in *Revelation* 14:20.

For the past quarter of a century, since the fall of the Soviet Union, Russian military power has experienced a literal rusting away of its nuclear submarines and has become outdated in its land forces. Yet under Vladimir Putin, who seeks to rebuild Russian authority as a power to be reckoned with, a final fulfilment of the Divine 'battle axe' command may be approaching.

This concerns the growing siege in Palestine of the Jewish Israeli State which has not borne the fruit of righteousness and praise among the people for 65 years since 1948. With the turmoil of Syria spreading and the nuclear challenge coming from any general escalation of conflict, these could bring Russia down as the catalyst of judgment upon the barren fig tree of the Jewish State.

It has been said that 'history repeats itself.' This has already been seen in this study, and it leads us to the end of the Babylonian succession, and the end of 50 Jubilees of Israel's warfare. Even so it is evident that the prophetic requirement of bringing in everlasting righteousness has not yet happened. There must be more to follow. As with the Map, the focal point changes as the journey proceeds. We are left with the King of the North, identified as Russia, acting to defeat Hitler's Germany, and having grabbed considerable territory. With the mind and the Maps the focal point is Russia . . . Russia honours the God of Force. We have seen on our News Programmes how they deal with opposition from Chechen rebels, and in the Balkans and Georgia we saw they will divide anyone's land for gain.

To resist the Kremlin just at the point of seizing such a prize will cause an all out response. The act of passing over may well mean not aircraft as before but intercontinental ballistic missiles. "He shall enter . . . the glorious land" implies that their plans will be well advanced before implementation of this Western counter attack, and several countries are shown as looking with favour on the Russian move.

We need to see from whom 'Tidings from the East & North' come. Going to our World Atlas, we find maps of the Polar Regions, look at the Northern Pole, and see what countries are both North and East of Russia. East is in an anticlockwise direction on the polar map. To the East therefore is Alaska,USA, and Canada. But to the North it is even more impressive. If you take a ruler and pass one end across Russia and rotating the middle of the ruler on the Pole, the other end will pass over Alaska, Canada across the Atlantic and Britain. All of this is both North & East of Russia the Bering Straits being the divide of East and West. It must be fairly obvious where the 'Troublesome tidings' come from, and that it is the West starting to take belated action to stop the Russian advance.

But Russia is an opportunist, and is waiting for the right moment. With patience they develop their strength. For the time being it is still Germany that is king of the North, recovered from the cost of World War II, and enjoying its newfound strength in the eurozone.

In the meantime Germany has assumed a leading role in Europe, and having had France as its favoured partner in coercing other Europeans to follow their lead, now has the strength of the Euro in its hands, numerous other countries experiencing the weakness of the Euro, simply because the single currency is unsuitable for varied economies and cultures, causing them severe debt problems, most especially Greece, and others not far behind.

Using its newfound power it has realigned with Italy instead of France, so that there is now a partnership of Germany and Italy heading up the destiny of Europe. This is a very bad omen, as some with memories of events in the 20th century, will recall, twice it was that Europe and the World was plunged into war by the Berlin/Rome Axis.

Using its newfound wealth by control of eurozone, Germany is cultivating allies in the Middle East, by providing armaments to the small Middle East States. The purpose of this is to create a friendly buffer zone against the aspirations of Iran, that has intentions to be the most powerful, a 'king of the South.'

Danger Ahead!

We have noted earlier that with the end of World War II, the period of Israel's 50 Jubilees of warfare was complete. Whose battle then is this? It is none other than the Lord's Great Day. The forces of this world, controlled by anti-God material power, are set to take by force God's Holy City, and destroy His Holy (separate) People. This will be among the most decisive moments of the Ages, as Joel tells us (3:14-16), "Multitudes, multitudes in the valley of decision," that is to say the decisive place and time when the LORD Himself will show His enemies how battles are fought and won. At the same time He will be the Hope and Strength of the children of Israel.

Daniel's Vision tells us very little about this event, its purpose only to give the Sealed Vision. The Seal being effective through the series of seemingly false starts, all of which are not false at all, but could not be deciphered before the events they represent took place. There is no need to encrypt the message any more as the events that surround the return of The Lord Jesus are openly described elsewhere. We are left with Michael the Archangel standing up to minimise the troubles of God's People that will be severe.

Deliverance is promised to the faithful. Help in preparing for the end times is on its way. Not part of Daniel's message, but relevant to it. Read *Matthew* 24:31, "And he shall send his angels with a great sound of a trumpet, and they shall gather together his elect from the four winds [global conflict], from one end of heaven to the other."

Chapter 12

12:1. And at that time shall Michael stand up, the great prince which standeth for the children of thy people: and there shall be a time of trouble, such as never was since there was a nation even to that same time: and at that time thy people shall be delivered, every one that shall be found written in the book.

Here we have the assurance that despite the sufferings of His people God is in command and has taken steps to reduce that suffering, and to rescue everyone who is faithful to Him, having their names recorded in the Lamb's Book of Life, of which our Lord Jesus is the custodian, see *Philippians* 4:3, and condemnation for those whose names are NOT entered, *Revelation* 13:6-10 & 20:15.

12:2-6. And many of them that sleep in the dust of the earth shall awake, some to everlasting life, and some to shame and everlasting contempt.

And they that be wise shall shine as the brightness of the firmament; and they that turn many to righteousness as the stars for ever and ever.

But thou, O Daniel, shut up the words, and seal the book, even to the time of the end: many shall run to and fro, and knowledge shall be increased.

Then I Daniel looked, and, behold, there stood other two, the one on this side of the bank of the river, and the other on that side of the bank of the river.

And one said to the man clothed in linen, which was upon the waters of the river, How long shall it be to the end of these wonders?

We go straight into the Resurrection, which implies that at a point not specified within these troubles Christ will Return and He will bring in 'Everlasting Righteousness,' and we will not need to ask, 'how long,' and Jerusalem or ZION, the City of Peace, which throughout its long history it has seldom been, will become by God's Grace, because He has not forgotten it, "ZION . . . A CITY NOT FORSAKEN."

Things will never be the same again! But we are not there yet.

> *12:7.   And I heard the man clothed in linen, which was upon the waters of the river, when he held up his right hand and his left hand unto heaven, and sware by him that liveth for ever that it shall be for a time, times, and an half; and when he shall have accomplished to scatter the power of the holy people, all these things shall be finished.*

The time, times, and an half, is exactly half of the seven times of punishment for Israel's sins, and is 1260 years. He is standing in the middle of the river, at the halfway point of 2520 years. As this brings us to the conclusion, he is symbolically at the midpoint of that punishment or chastisement, and indicating towards its completion.

At which time Israel/Britain and her associated nations will be in the process of having their power scattered or broken. That may mean to have lost both the spiritual and political will to resist the combined inroads of globalisation, terrorism and Satanism.

> *12:8-10.   And I heard, but understood not: then said I, O my Lord, what shall be the end of these things?*
>
> *And he said, Go thy way, Daniel: for the words are closed up and sealed till the time of the end.*
>
> *Many shall be purified, and made white, and tried; but the wicked shall do wickedly: and none of the wicked shall understand; but the wise shall understand.*

Even Daniel did not understand the angelic vision completely, simply because the time to understand it was still far off. But in the intervening time, many will be faithful in their witness for God and His Gospel, some of whom will be tried even to being martyrs for their faith and understanding; but the wicked who choose to persist in wickedness are barred from understanding the Mysteries of God.

12:11-13. And from the time that the daily sacrifice shall be taken away, and the abomination that maketh desolate set up, there shall be a thousand two hundred and ninety days.

Blessed is he that waiteth, and cometh to the thousand three hundred and five and thirty days.

But go thou thy way till the end be: for thou shalt rest, and stand in thy lot at the end of the days.

Further chronological markers on the day for a year scale: 1290 is a number representing desolation, and is connected to Islam. From AD 634 when Omar became their powerful leader until the collapse of the Caliphate in 1924 is 1290 years, an event probably contributed to by the failure of their Palestinian campaign of World War I.

1335 is the number in the Islamic calendar for the year AD 1917. Egyptian coins that year had both dates on them, 1335 was in Arabic figures, 1917 in English. That December Jerusalem was surrendered to the British and Colonial forces, and marks the fact that Islamic influences will be involved in the events at the close of this troubled era. Note that it was only Jerusalem that was surrendered, the Turkish/Islamic forces were never defeated, in the same way there was an armistice in 1918 without the defeat of Germany, although some called it a Victory it was only a cease fire. Both forces have in their own time and way made a comeback. Germany in World War II, and later, Islam in the form of terrorist attacks.

The Blessing for the Holy City was the release from Islamic power placing it under a Christian power that was also the representative of latter day Israel under the leadership of a descendant of King David, not to the Jews. It marked the end of the 2520 years punishment from its capture and destruction by Nebuchadne**zar**.

It is curious to see that the **'ZAR'** final syllable of his name has been used in the titles of Heads of State to the Roman Empire and onwards by others; as in Belsha**zzar,** Cae**sar,** T**zar** and the Kai**ser.**

As for Daniel, he will be back to play his part with the returning Jesus.

Having looked at the 70 weeks Prophecy and its accompanying Sealed Vision, albeit briefly, let us look further at the present and approaching crisis. We have witnessed the completion of its chronological periods, and we have been informed to expect an advance by Russia, into the Holy Land, that will precipitate, or be party to, World Conflict. The first phase of this took place in the late 1940s when hoards of Jewish folk from Eastern Europe and Russia forced themselves into Palestine.

We are in an interim period, during which things are happening and for which most are totally unprepared. The danger of the Russian advance may be realised as diplomatic efforts are often of an appeasing nature in the hope that Russia will not think it needful to start any trouble. While this seems to keep things quiet the Enemy has other plans afoot. As our attention is diverted on peace keeping missions and racism and immigration legal and illegal, our Constitution is being demolished, with hardly a word being said about it by either Government or Opposition. Our attention is diverted from the real power struggles that are going on.

On 11 September 2001 terror, sudden death and disaster in New York and Washington, on a scale never before seen in so short a time. The consequences of this atrocity will be with us for some time. Then there was the terror in London on 7 July 2005, followed in 2006 by exposure and security measures because of an alleged plot to destroy aircraft. Many are troubled at these ongoing and seemingly insoluble problems. Those who put their trust for the future in political initiatives or military power have little comfort.

Remember, "the Eternal God is thy refuge, and underneath are the everlasting arms: and he shall thrust out the enemy from before thee" (*Deuteronomy* 33).

Let us be thankful to our God who raised up Daniel and the other Prophets to give us guidance in these times, and to Jesus our Saviour and Redeemer who gave us the Revelation himself, and all Scripture by inspiration of His Holy Spirit, in which we have the Promise of His Return in Power and Glory.

FURTHER READING

The Royal House of Britain an Enduring Dynasty
by W.M.H. Milner

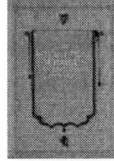

Moses in the Hieroglyphs by G. Berkeley

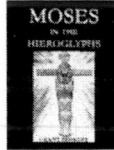

Revelation Unlocked by M.S. Jarvis

The Post-Captivity Names of Israel
by Rev. W. Pascoe Goard

The Names of God by Rev. W. Pascoe Goard

All books from Covenant Publishing